SPIRITUAL SURVIVAL HANDBOOK

FOR CROSS-CULTURAL WORKERS

BY DR. ROBERT S. MILLER

Spiritual Survival Handbook for Cross-Cultural Workers
By Dr. Robert S. Miller

Unless otherwise indicated, Bible quotations are taken from The Holy Bible: Today's New International Version (TNIV). Copyright © 2005 by the International Bible Society.

Editor: Caryn Pederson
Cover Design: Jason LaBombard
Interior Design: Carissa Sheehan

Printed in the USA. For worldwide distribution.

BottomLine Media is a ministry of Pioneers that exists to celebrate the "bottom line" of God's promise to Abraham that He would bless all nations through him.

Pioneers mobilizes teams to glorify God among unreached peoples by initiating church-planting movements in partnership with local churches.

For information on Pioneers and to shop for more BottomLine resources, visit *pioneers.org.*

BottomLine Media
An Imprint of Pioneers
10123 William Carey Drive
Orlando, FL 32832
(800) 755-7284

FOREWORD

All of us who are involved in ministry can recall many tests, trials and attacks that we've experienced. These attacks come in many different forms. I can remember days when I literally called out, "Lord, please have mercy on me!" On other occasions, the attacks and dangers are much more subtle, like the frog in the kettle.

Use of warfare terminology and metaphors is not as common in Christian culture today. Perhaps they are not considered "politically correct." We do not often sing songs like "Dare to be a Daniel." However, the reality is that the Scriptures are full of battle terminology. Every believer, and especially those in ministry or trying to establish gospel beachheads in unreached cultures, is engaged in a titanic spiritual struggle.

Against this backdrop, it is absolutely crucial that we equip ourselves for the work to which we've been called. Here's where I find Dr. Robert Miller's *Spiritual Survival Handbook for Cross-Cultural Workers* to be so incredibly applicable and powerful. Some of the thoughts that came to my mind as I worked through the material were:

These concepts fit perfectly with what we do in Pioneers. This is exactly what all our people around the world need at this time.

This book is called the Spiritual Survival Handbook, *and it does a superb job of addressing the issue of spiritual survival. However, in my mind it does far more than that. It goes well beyond survival to the issue of fruitfulness. I find myself thinking these are exactly the foundational principles that lead to spiritual fruitfulness in our lives and ministries. It*

3

is one thing to go to the ends of the earth and survive. It is another matter to flourish and be fruitful despite the onslaught of enemy fire. The Lord's will for us is to "go and bear fruit, fruit that will last."

I wish I had better understood all these principles years ago. I wish I had written this book! I could have saved myself considerable heartache and wasted effort.

Everyone in Pioneers should thoughtfully read through this material at least twice a year. I think it would do wonders for our workers in 90 countries to reflect on these foundational concepts and to renew their faith, discipline and perspective.

Whoever wrote this has a lot of missions experience! The words hit home so pointedly to the kinds of experiences and pressures that my wife and I faced frequently in our years of service in a Muslim culture.

I'm amazed by the "density" of this book. It is not a long book, and in some ways it is an easy read, except that you have to stop, think and reflect frequently. Every page moves fast and is packed with life-changing insight.

I fully expect that the Spiritual Survival Handbook for Cross-Cultural Workers *becomes one of a small number of key handbooks that will be used widely in Pioneers to guide and encourage our workers.*

We need to multiply this teaching. I am eager to see it made available, not only to Pioneers' global workforce, but to workers with other mission agencies as well. Along with our church-planting training, our InTent leadership development program and our Clarion team-building modules, I believe the Spiritual Survival Workshops will become an enduring and profoundly helpful dimension of our missionary training strategy.

Steve Richardson
President of Pioneers-USA

PROLOGUE

Imagine you are trekking the Himalayas with a group of mountain climbers. Supplies are running low and impending weather threatens your survival. You gather together to gain input from your guide. There is no time for pleasantries. Rather, every minute is filled with key, strategic discussions. Each person listens carefully knowing that the information might mean the difference between life and death.

Take what you read in this book and place it within that context. The main presupposition of this work is that the fight for survival is real. Missionaries today undoubtedly serve in the spiritually desolate areas of our world. If not careful, the elements they face each day could cost them their lives or their ministries. Radical obedience to the Great Commission brings with it certain dangers.

Every year, hundreds of new missionaries set out for service among the world's unreached peoples. Some are familiar with the principles of spiritual warfare, but many are not. Not all understand the dynamics of power and authority structures, or endure intense criticism well. Few know how to establish and maintain healthy boundaries.

Nearly everyone enters ministry with glaring blind spots such as these. This is true of any profession, but in ministry the spiritual dynamics are so persistent and intense that one mistake can be lethal. The wilderness is not the place to practice spiritual exercises for the first time. Yet thousands of new missionaries go bravely to deserts or urban jungles unaware that they have an enemy.

Imagine a hiker seeking to scale Mount Everest with every piece of equipment except crampons. He may be the most fit member of his expedition, but without appropriate equipment to keep his footing, he may not make it.

It is not simply a matter of gifting. It is also a matter of equipping.

I do not intend to be melodramatic when I speak of surviving in ministry. Many gifted missionaries fall. Not a week goes by without mission agencies speaking with members who have lost their passion, those whose family or team relationships are under significant strain or others whose kids are acting out due to the stresses in the family. Left alone, these can be the precursors to moral failure, abuse, addiction or other actions that would require people to leave the mission field.

Do you hear the voices behind such heartache? Have you heard their stories?

> *When you're working in a place where you aren't seeing any fruit, you feel like you can keep at it when your team is strong. Because of the isolation from other supportive relationships, often your team is your family, your best friends, your church and your coworkers, and so the breakdown of that team impacts every area of life. I thought I'd be in the country for five to ten years or more. I had no intention of leaving. The dissolving of our team brought so much loss—loss of relationship, a place of belonging, of ministry hopes and dreams. When those dreams have all been shattered, then what?*

> — a former missionary in Europe

> *My family and I were the first with our mission to live in this region of the world. The locals were known for chewing up missionaries and spitting them out, but despite that, we did well in our cultural adaptation and language learning. Things were going well, but we were very isolated. We had no church; we had no team. In a culture of millions, there were only a couple of dozen white faces, and my family had five of them. Over time, my normally bubbly wife became less and less interested in leaving our home because*

when she left the house, she was treated as a celebrity by some and a sex object by others. When we finally did get teammates, we didn't connect well with them. In fact, we had conflict. We left the area after our first term thoroughly intending to go back, and got caught in a political uprising on our way home. Mayhem ruled. Shopping malls were looted and burned. Cars were destroyed—and we were within 15 minutes of being caught in it all. We were never debriefed from that experience, and shortly afterward, the conflict we experienced with our teammates came to a head. This conflict combined with the isolation, the uprising and a lack of support from my supervisor led me to resign. I felt like a failure. Years of my life seemed lost because so few people speak the language I had mastered. There was the loss of feeling useful and the loss of what could have been.

— a former missionary in Asia

We came to the field ready to plant a church. Within four months, we realized our team leaders were wolves in sheep's clothing. They lied to get funds. They manipulated their supporters. They cheated us. They had home issues that bordered on criminal. We had to partner with our organization to discipline them, only to have the organization demote them and place them back on our team. Obviously this didn't work. After dealing with their passive aggression and overt attacks, we asked our organization to let them go. They did, but the family stayed a few miles from where we were and planted their own church. We also suffered severe financial issues stemming from trusting someone back home. We lost our credit. And after dealing with another couple whose marriage was floundering, we had a hard time concentrating on actually planting a church. With the added issues of our children crying at school (learning a new language), overt spiritual attack on our family and the constant strain of culture learning, it is no surprise we were diagnosed with PTSD (post traumatic stress disorder) after our first nine months on the field.

— a former missionary in Europe

Though the number of disheartening testimonies from missionaries and ex-missionaries seems to be growing at an exponential rate, the harsh relational terrain of ministry has existed for thousands of years. Jesus was misrepresented (Luke 11:15-20), rejected (John 1:11), betrayed by a co-worker (Luke 22:47-48), disowned by a close companion (Mark 14:66-72), falsely accused (Matthew 26:59-60) and deserted by His friends when He needed them the most (Matthew 26:36-46). The Apostle Paul dealt with many of the same challenges. Our Lord warns us, "No servant is greater than his master. If they persecuted me, they will persecute you also" (John 15:20). We must prepare for these challenges if we are to survive.

This book is organized around seven primary words that I wish I had heard at the beginning of my ministry career—seven words that speak to seven imposing obstacles in missions. I do not claim to offer a final word on any of these topics. In fact, I hope and pray you will want to learn more about each of them, and where possible I've tried to point you in the right direction. A survival guide, by definition, is concise and quickly zeroes in on the urgent, laying the groundwork so that one day you can think well beyond surviving to thriving in the ministry to which you have been called. It is my hope that by passing this advice to you now, you will be able to realistically assess the challenging and adventurous terrain that stretches out before you. Lift up your eyes and look upon this land! It is a land filled not just with danger, but also with great opportunity.

This handbook is my offering to you, and not for mere survival, but for victorious, anointed service to the King of Kings, Jesus Christ.

TABLE OF CONTENTS

Innumerable missionaries have lost their way by trying to minister in their own strength, only to find themselves burned out and lacking motivation to continue. Apart from intimate fellowship with the Lord, there is no chance of survival.

A strong sense of identity and a formidable reservoir of inner courage are required if a missionary is to survive the complex and intense world of ministry.

Casual mindsets about the strategies and traps of the enemy have led many missionaries to the brink of destruction.

The terrain of ministry is full of life-giving opportunities. It is also full of danger. Become a student of the wilderness environment in which your ministry will either rise or fall.

Whether it is because of an affair, ministry burnout or foolish communication, thousands of missionaries have shipwrecked their careers by being careless in the domain of boundaries.

Every year missionary teams crumble as a result of the misuse of power, poor management style or a lack of team mentality. Do not think for a minute that any missionary is immune from this challenge.

The old adage is true: If we aim at nothing, that is precisely what we will hit. Many missionaries and their teams don't survive because of lack of vision and purpose.

A Desert Survival Kit
The Identity School for Christian Ministry
For Team Leaders

KNOW YOUR GOD

What's wrong with me? *I* wondered. After seven years of leading a team in Asia, my polished image as a good team leader was showing some serious wear-and-tear around the edges. I fought hard to maintain my reputation, openly criticizing others' strategies and feeling superior in my theological views. Outwardly I endeared myself to national leaders; inwardly I had come to despise them. And then the storm began. A national leader, once my student and close friend, slandered my good name. Two promising visa plans fell through. Subtle, unnamed fears began to keep me awake at night. One of my team members was stabbed: I can't let him die on my watch. The next day my house was broken into when my son was home alone: I have to guarantee his safety. When this final crisis came I couldn't face it. My world caved in around me; I was burnt out beyond recognition. A couple months later my overseas ministry career came to a crying halt. Where had I gone wrong?

— a former missionary in Southeast Asia

If our blessed Lord Who is our perfect example in everything… found it necessary, or desirable, thus to hold unhurried and responsive fellowship with the Heavenly Father, what presumptuous and alarming folly for us to assume that in these busy, noisy lives of ours, and in the midst of the dangerous cross currents of the modern world, we can do without this truly Christ-like practice.

—John R. Mott, founder and 32-year chair
of the Student Volunteer Movement

So much of what I have learned about survival in ministry is based on the following statement: "Inward before outward, secret before public." You must win the battle within your own person if you are to survive in ministry. Success in this inner terrain requires a commitment of the heart and a renewing of the mind. Start your training here in the secret places.

Let the river flow into your heart.

There is a river that proceeds from fellowship with the Spirit, a river that waters your thirsty life. The flow of this river is dependent on your heart's posture before the Lord. A subtle shift will cause the flow to pause or even stop. Without that life-giving river, your heart will become a desert.

We cannot give what we do not have. There are times when we attempt to minister apart from this flow. Such a condition is so prevalent that we can become accustomed to it and think it is normal. After all, no one is perfect; we're all human. But the sobering truth is that a missionary that is evangelizing, discipling or church planting apart from abiding in the Spirit may as well be playing the role of a missionary in a Hollywood film. We cannot give what we do not have. Without the living water, there is no living, vital ministry.

This survival key is in some sense the most important one of all, which is why it comes first. In fact, it can't be isolated from any of the other keys. The capacity to know yourself, your enemy, the terrain and your mission, as well as your ability to respect boundaries and to lead effectively are inextricably tied to your relationship with God.

Everything is about your walk with the Lord. Is your heart alive with a flowing river or is it dead?

How long does it take for a heart to become an arid desert? Not years and not even months. Guard your heart daily.

The river of fellowship with your Lord and Savior is the key to your life and your ministry; everything else takes second place. This priority must be reflected in your daily schedule, your weekly agenda and in your yearly calendar.

The Daily Discipline

The very minute your eyes open for the first time in the morning, dedicate yourself to the service of the Lord. Before your feet touch the floor, before you rise from your bed, commit yourself to the Lord's purposes for the day.

Do not listen to people who say this special appointment with the Lord can occur anytime of the day. Do not rationalize saying, "I'm not a morning person, so I'll have my time with the Lord in the evening." You *must* begin your day by being alone with God.

I schedule early appointments with people, but my first appointment is always with Jesus Christ.

I must spend time with Him. Not just five or ten minutes. I must linger with Him. I need the living water. I need to know Him and to be known by Him. If I forego this priority-one appointment, my heart

The river of fellowship with your Lord and Savior is the key to your life and your ministry.

will become a desert and I will die. When we forego our time with the Lord, we are choosing to take our eyes off the river of life and go our own way. It is both subtle and dangerous. No Christian can afford to lose this early morning battle. No missionary can lose sight of these early morning decisions.

Linger in the morning with your Lord. Though the Bible is an essential ingredient of this appointment with Jesus, this time is not about Bible study. Schedule other times in your day for the discipline of study. This time is about relationship. It is a time of friendship, of lingering.

I start this morning time on my knees. This position reminds me that Jesus is Lord (and I am not). Kneeling reminds me of my desperate need for my Savior's intervention in my life. I may read a psalm. Often I will read it out loud. I find that I need to get out of my head, break the silence and use my voice and my body. I enter His courts with thanksgiving and praise. Do not be concerned about feelings. Emotional satisfaction will come and go. God will bless you for your consistency and your earnest desire to meet with Him. When we seek Him with all our hearts, He will be found by us (Jeremiah 29: 11-13).

After a time of kneeling, I often walk with Him. I go outside or even just move around the room. I have come to understand the simple truth that my physical body wants to get comfortable. I know how easy it is to be lulled into religious exercise and forget that I am actually meeting with a Person—the King of Kings!

> *I have come to understand the simple truth that my physical body wants to get comfortable.*

In this regard, we are all the same. There is a dominion we must exert over our physical bodies if we are to become mature disciples of our Lord. "Run in such a way as to get the prize. Everyone who competes in the games goes into strict training. They do it to get a crown that will not last; but we do it to get a crown that will last forever. Therefore I do not run like a man running aimlessly; I do not fight like a man beating the air. No, I beat my body and make it my slave so that after I have preached to others, I myself will not be disqualified for the prize" (1 Corinthians 9:24-27). Practice praying in the Spirit. Practice singing a new song to the Lord. Practice pouring yourself out for Him in praise and adoration.

Then practice listening. Ask the Lord to speak His heart to your heart. Give Him permission to shine His light in every area of your life. Pray this: "Whatever You desire to say, Lord—whether it is an encouragement, an exhortation, a prophecy or a rebuke—I want to hear it! I need to hear it!"

During such listening times, all types of distractions will come to you. Some of the distractions are external (the phone, the weather, a person passing by, a sound). However, the most persistent distractions are internal (looping thought cycles, the "to do" list of ministry, hunger pangs, carnal desires, feelings, boredom). Do not beat yourself up over these interruptions; this is simply the terrain where you must fight for survival each morning. Don't despair. Realize that this is indeed a matter of life and death and that you can be victorious in the name of Jesus!

Some days you will totally overcome distraction and find yourself in sweet fellowship with the Spirit. Other days, it will seem like an uphill battle from start to finish. You are being strengthened in both the easy and the hard

You are being strengthened in both the easy and the hard times.

times. Engage in fighting through the distraction. You are weight lifting in the spiritual realm. Over time, your muscles will develop. God will give you power and teach you techniques for waiting on the Lord (for this is what you are practicing daily). The daily workout causes you to become tenacious in your spirit. This is a rare characteristic among North American Christians. In our culture, if something is hard, we give up too easily. We need to learn from our brothers and sisters in the Third World—especially those who are being persecuted for their faith. They are tenacious; they have learned how to stand in the storm. God wants you to be tenacious! The Holy Spirit is calling you to His daily training ground, teaching you perseverance.

Traditionally, in many Christian circles, this daily personal appointment has been called a "quiet time." Anyone who has walked with the Lord for an extended period of time knows that it is difficult to become quiet. It is a raging war, and the enemy wants you to grow weary in trying.

How would you design an important meeting with the most respected person in your life? You would eliminate as many distractions as possible. You would prepare for that meeting and do everything in your power to make the most of this special opportunity. Have that mindset with your morning appointment with Jesus.

The Weekly Discipline

Along with your daily quiet times with the Lord, see that you have an extended time with Him every week. Practice solitude. If there is any way, do this in some sort of wilderness.[1] Rise early in the morning and don't return to your normal routine until after lunch. Take only your Bible and your journal. Find a secluded place where you can hide away. It is best if this place is away from your home and your primary ministry locations, but if your host culture won't allow that, still "get away" in some fashion. Try a friend's living room, or even noise-cancelling headphones. (One missionary finds these very helpful not for listening to music or sermons, but for practicing solitude in a home with young children.) Better yet, take a hike. Discover new secret places. Don't worry if it is raining or cold. Consider Jesus in the wilderness for forty days. Think about the millions of brothers and sisters in the world today who are being tortured daily because of their faith in Christ. You can survive six hours in less than perfect conditions. Howard Macey writes: "The spiritual life cannot be made suburban. It is always frontier, and we who live in it must accept and rejoice that it remains untamed."[2]

Through this discipline, you are learning to depend on God alone.

We need to get back to our roots. God calls us to the wilderness—to God's sanctuary. When I walk in the mountains, I become very aware of how big the mountain is and how small I am. I gain a deeper appreciation for the Mountain Maker. In nature, we can re-capture the wonder that has been lost under artificial lighting and the controlled environments of automobiles, computers and restaurants.

Words, written and spoken, surround us all the time. We are inundated with words, but are unfamiliar with, perhaps even intimidated by, silence. Mountains will speak, but with very few words. Nature knows how to bow before the Creator. Our artificial world is all about self-expression—all mouth and no ears.

You will be tempted to take a friend with you on these excursions.

Unless there is no way around it, fight that temptation. Your wilderness time is a training ground for you and the Holy Spirit. In these hours, you will experience a wrestling within yourself that exposes weakness and depletion. But while you are experiencing a variety of frustrating feelings, the Lord will be strengthening your ankles as you walk this trail. You are being trained and conditioned for battle. Through this discipline, you are learning to depend on God alone.

I have met only a handful of people who operate out of the Spirit's strength. The Spirit is delighted to fill every man and woman who is rightly postured before Him. The moment I begin to fuel my life with my own power, I have lost sight of the spiritual reality that apart from the Lord, I can do nothing (John 15:5). The morning battle and the weekly time away, when operating according to the Spirit, establish this truth deep within our souls and cause the river to flow from Him to us. When we find that sweet communion, much power is available for ministry to others. Without this flow, we are like a broken water fountain in the park on a hot day—unable to offer what people really need.

> Inner reconciliation is a prerequisite to being an ambassador of reconciliation.

The Discipline of Personal Retreats

Finally, I recommend you get away for a personal overnight retreat at least four times a year. (These should last at least 24 hours.) Keep it simple, remembering that this practice is not about luxury or comfort. It is about equipping. These disciplines frustrate the carnal nature and strengthen the spiritual nature, so don't be surprised if you feel like you're in a battle. You are.

Prepare for your personal retreats. Ask the Lord ahead of time, "What is it that you want me to consider? What is it that you're showing me about my heart, my family, my ministry?" Come to your retreat with a specific question for the Lord or a specific area of study. Consider also fasting during part or all of your personal retreats. The old proverb is true: "If you aim at nothing, that's precisely what you'll hit." So write down the purpose of your retreat. Of course, that purpose might and often does change. The Lord might lead you in a completely different direction. Be prepared for a new direction, but come prepared to make effective use of your time away. I believe the Lord appreciates our passion to discover and to ask.

You may be astounded by my emphasis on time alone with God. Why would so much of a missionary's time be given to the inward journey? What about other people? What about the "to do" list or outreach visits or the organization of the ministry? Just remember: Inward before outward; secret before public.

If our Lord needed alone time with His Father, how much more so do we?

This is the example that Jesus set for us. The disciples often found Him spending time alone with His Abba on a mountain or in the wilderness. They watched Him depart for hours at a time or overnight, and then saw Him return refreshed and renewed in vision. If our Lord needed alone time with His Father, how much more so do we?

Inner reconciliation is a prerequisite to being an ambassador of reconciliation. In order to have something to give people when you are with them, you must spend time alone in the river. You need to be "wet" with the Spirit when people brush up against you. They should be able to sense that you've been soaking in His Presence. Don't towel off! Don't make yourself "presentable." Drip His Presence on the floor of the kitchen, on the carpet of your office, and on the streets of the city to which you've been called.

I have set a basic structure before you that, if followed, can assist you in keeping communion with the Lord. Practice the classical spiritual disciplines consistently. View them not as taskmasters, but as allies in living out the abundant life that God desires for you. When operating according to the Spirit, they will enable Christ's presence to flow freely from Him to you to others.

Let the river renew your mind.

The river flowing from God's Word and God's Spirit must not just irrigate our hearts, but also our thinking. In his book, *The Three Battlegrounds*, Francis Frangipane reminds us that the blood of Jesus Christ was spilled at a place called "Golgotha," which means "the place of the skull." A fierce battle is still raging in "the place of the skull" (in the realm of our thoughts). We must win this fight by finding and putting to death all anti-biblical perspectives. The Bible tells us not "to be conformed to the pattern of this world," but to be transformed by the renewing of our minds (Romans 12:2).

How does the river (God's word, God's spirit) flow into our minds? Every piece of information I retrieve must first pass through my "mind-skin"[3] (my personal system of adopted life paradigms). Every emotion, thought, imagination, conviction, etc.—is shaped and manipulated by this filter before I even begin consciously processing the information. If my mind-skin is not aligned to the Word of God, no matter how hard I try, I will not be able to enter into God's perspective concerning all that is going on inside me, around me and in the world. But if I allow the Holy Spirit to pour over my mind-skin, the very way I process can be transformed and my mind can be renewed (properly aligned to the principles in the Word of God).

Some examples of mind-skin constructs:

- Some people see the glass half-full; others see it half-empty (regardless of which glass catches their eyes).

- Some people crave change; others fear it (regardless of the change that is occurring).

- Some, because of past wounds, find it hard to trust people in authority. Others, because of their good experiences with authority figures, find it easier to trust (regardless of whether or not the present authority figure is trustworthy or not).

Our mind-skins are made up of unconscious patterns that we've adopted in order to make sense of the world and survive in it. We can remain in subjection to these unconscious patterns or we can cry out for God's river to pour over us.

When God's river flows into our mind-skins, a miracle begins to happen: our perspective changes even if our circumstances remain the same. When our mind-skins begin to align with God's principles, paradigm shifts begin to occur.

> *I can't* becomes *I can.*
> *It will never change* becomes *Anything is possible.*
> *Worthless* becomes *Invaluable.*
> *Just getting by* becomes *Aspiring and achieving.*

God's thinking is not at all like our thinking (Isaiah 55:8). We see an acorn; He sees an oak tree. We see a closed box; He sees an open lid. We see our worthlessness; He sees our great potential in Christ.[4]

Jesus said, "No one pours new wine into old wineskins. If he does, the wine will burst the skins and both the wine and the wineskins will be ruined" (Mark 2:22). Is your mind-skin old and rigid or is it new and flexible? This is an important question because the way you process information can make or break your ministry.

Remember, every bit of information must first pass through your unconscious paradigm grid. If your mind-skin interprets disagreement as rejection, then you will see honest challenge as disaffirmation or betrayal. If your mind-skin interprets change as uncomfortable and frightening, then you will unconsciously struggle with change of any kind. If your mind-skin registers every conflict as a personal attack, you will distance yourself from every person with whom you share an argument.

Moving Forward

Is there a path to freedom? The transformation that we long for comes by the renewing of our minds. The Lord has a different perspective on things. We need His eyes. We need His way of thinking. Ask Jesus to transform the way you process information. The rigid expectation that you and I have unconsciously adopted in order to survive must give way to new, flexible mind-skins. If we ask Him and if we are willing to do all He directs us to do, our Lord will gladly pour His river into us!

CHAPTER 1 STUDY QUESTIONS

1. In what life areas do you most feel the fight for survival? What are you willing to do to equip yourself to survive this journey? Write a prayer to your Father expressing your willingness.

2. Ask the Spirit to help you examine yourself. How much are you working in your own effort? Repent of this. Admit it to one of your teammates. How much are you working in the energy given by the life-giving water of Jesus? Believe and receive this.

3. Do you "linger" with Jesus every day in friendship with him? What prevents you from doing so? Do you "kneel," "move," and "listen" when you're meeting with him (p. 13-15)?

4. Ask God to help you fill in your "calendar" (below) with a plan for meeting with him regularly and consistently. Share your plan with a teammate who will pray for you to follow through—motivated by Jesus and relying on the Spirit's power.

	Daily	Weekly	Yearly
When?			
Where?			
How?			

Those who listen to the word but do not do what it says are like people who look at their faces in a mirror and, after looking at themselves, go away and immediately forget what they look like. —James 1:23-24

KNOW YOURSELF

In America, I'd been a highly competent and independent career woman. Because of my confidence in my roles as worker and friend, I demanded little, shied from the limelight and seldom required affirmation. Then I moved to a country that routinely dismisses women as ignorant and unimportant outside of motherhood. I was crushed! I found myself trying again and again to prove my worth—to the guard, the office manager, the shopkeeper. I felt foolish and frustrated as my feeble attempts failed to overturn their worldview. Over time, I realized that unmet needs were driving my madcap efforts. I needed to have my personhood valued, my gifts affirmed and my ministry efforts recognized. I saw that my sense of self was tightly wound up in what I did back home, and that held no value here. I had to admit that my understanding of my identity and worth in Christ was seriously lacking the substance and depth necessary to navigate this spiritually hostile environment.

— a former missionary in Central Asia

There is a universal saying to the effect that it is when men are off in the wilds that they show themselves as they really are. As in the case with the majority of proverbs, there is much truth in it, for without the minor comforts of life to smooth things down, and with even the elemental necessities more or less problematic, the inner man has an unusual opportunity of showing himself—and he is not always attractive. A man may be a pleasant companion when you always meet him clad in dry clothes, and certain of substantial meals at regulated intervals, but the same cheery individual may be a different person when you are both on half rations, eaten cold and have been drenched for three days—sleeping from utter exhaustion, cramped and wet.

— Kermit Roosevelt, son of Theodore Roosevelt[5]

God is doing a work in me
He's walking through my rooms and halls
Checking every corner
Tearing down the unsafe walls
Letting in the light
And I am working hard,
To clean my house and set it straight…

— Sara Groves, "Help Me Be New"

Have you ever found yourself in a situation where, all of a sudden, you experience much more emotion than the context warrants? A moment before, everything was normal. But then, something happened and now raw feelings are flooding into the moment like a waterfall. What was it? A specific word? A particular facial expression? A subtle dismissal? What was the trigger and where did it send you?

In order to be liberated in our ministry to others, we must find a measure of liberation in our own selves. We must do the inner work, we must find the buttons that, when pushed, cause us to react instead of respond.

Are you willing to look in the mirror? Survival key #2 is all about personal discovery. This battlefield requires great courage and perseverance. Are you willing to look into the mirror? Are you willing to ask the Holy Spirit to reveal the deep script written on the fabric of your heart? Proceed carefully and prayerfully in this terrain.

The Mirror

Those of us in ministry are extremely vulnerable to attack if we do not settle the issue of identity in the very core of our beings.

We must deal with the mirror or it will destroy us.

Every missionary should learn:

- How to be self-identified

- How to withstand betrayal and rejection

- How to disagree with a co-worker and still remain active in ministry with that person

- How to receive correction without being offended

The list could go on and on, but the main point is this: The Holy Spirit longs to establish a solid sense of self in every one of us. Talents, skills, charisma and training are all wonderful tools for ministry, but if we have not graduated from the identity school led by the Spirit of God, then all our ministry efforts are built on sinking sand. God's identity classes are held every day. They are twenty-four hours long. All the classes are practicums. We learn by watching our Teacher and following His example.

> *The Holy Spirit longs to establish a solid sense of self in every one of us.*

Are you interested in this school? Are you teachable? Do you really want to learn? If so, you are welcome to enroll in God's school, and He will gladly be your Teacher.

During His earthly ministry, Jesus had a solid sense of self. Neither the people praising Him nor those cursing Him altered His view of Himself and His mission. How did He walk through life in this manner? What was His secret? His identity was grounded not in the way people looked at Him, but in the way His Father looked at Him.

God wants each of us to look into the mirror and see ourselves through His eyes. Of course, if our eyes are not opened to seeing Jesus present with us, the mirror will be haunting. I cannot tell you how God will form your sense of self, but the following guidelines may prove helpful in the journey:

- We must surrender our lives entirely into the hands of our loving heavenly Father. We must build upon His promises and His love. A person's self-worth and identity cannot be built on the opinions of others.

- It is imperative to say no to any agenda besides allowing Christ's river to flow through our lives into the world.

- Addressing issues related to your family of origin is essential. Part of this work is learning about our unconscious contracts concerning trust, loyalty and love. It is imperative that we discover how our buttons get pushed, because believe me, they will get pushed.

- Inner healing and deliverance is another essential area to explore. The power to change is available in the name of the Lord Jesus. The Bible teaches that breakthroughs come by way of confession, repentance, taking back the ground in the name of Christ and complete surrender to His Lordship. Any demonic strongholds in our lives must be destroyed in this manner—strongholds of resentment, pride, lust or envy. The enemy will capitalize on any advantage he can find in our past, our character and our ways of relating to others.

Just as physical mirrors are used for the sake of external presentation, we need spiritual mirrors that reflect back to us our inner character and condition. These spiritual mirrors can emerge in various ways. They may come as we are reading His Word or while we are praying. God may reveal them through the community of faith (a prophecy or a word of counsel from a friend) to bring us insight about ourselves. He may also use circumstances or other people to hold up a mirror to our faces.

Not all mirrors offer a perfect reflection, and often our eyes do not see clearly even when they do.

A word of caution: Not all mirrors offer a perfect reflection, and often our eyes do not see clearly even when they do. Nevertheless, we must take courage to stand in front of spiritual mirrors when we are given the opportunity. God wants us to see our present condition so that when He changes us, we will rejoice all the more.

The Script

And now for the first time I knew what I had been doing. While I was reading, it had, once and again, seemed strange to me that the reading took so long; for the book was a small one. Now I knew that I had been reading it over and over—perhaps a dozen times. I would have read it forever, quick as I could, starting the first word again almost before the last was out of my mouth, if the judge had not stopped me. And the voice I read it in was strange to my ears. There was given to me a certainty that this, at last, was my real voice.

— C. S. Lewis, *Till We Have Faces*[6]

There is a script hidden deep in every person's heart; it is one's life story told from a personal perspective. It is composed of vows, fears and survival tactics—words that we have written on our own hearts with tears and dreams. The writing of this script began the first day of our lives and continues to this present moment. It is a concise expression of our deepest groanings. This script is our modus operandi; it governs our lives in ways we cannot fully understand.

A variety of topics are discussed within the script: how to survive emotional loss, how to handle deep disappointments, how to react when you feel you don't belong, etc. Under each of these headings, explicit instructions are offered to "remedy" the particular circumstance. When we are hard pressed and the pressure is on, our more superficial convictions give way to the deep patterns and entitlements of our written code of conduct.

> *The writing of this script began the first day of our lives and continues to this present moment.*

Here is the good news: There is *another script*. This one resides deep in God's heart. It is His prophetic word for your life, a word that speaks of your identity and destiny in Christ. This script describes us more beautifully than we can imagine. The prophetic script is all about our potential—God's dream for us—a magnificent, breathtaking and inspiring vision for our lives.

If the script is to be replaced, all of the ties that bind must be detached.

Though you have rehearsed your life script for years and years, it need not be your destiny. Do not allow it to rule you any longer. In the name of Jesus, set your natural script before the cross and ask the Lord to place in your heart the prophetic script He has written for you. Exchange one declaration for the other. Allow the Great Physician to minister deep and tender healing in the areas of identity and destiny. The more you are released on the inside, the more able you will be to extend Spirit-filled, anointed ministry to others.

Detaching the Tethers

The script's influence in our lives can be likened to tethers that extend from our hearts and attach to people, ideas and things. For some of us, the tethers have existed for such a long time that these attachments seem normal and right. But if the script is to be replaced, all of the ties that bind must be detached. This work is intensive; it doesn't happen overnight. But be encouraged: God is an excellent surgeon and He is able to set us free. He desires to release us into Spirit-filled ministry, but we must be willing to let go of these attachments and lay quietly on the operating table, entrusting ourselves fully to the One who called us into His service.

Some tethers that must be detached:

People's Opinions

With the Lord's help, detach the tether that causes you to cater to people's opinions. Replace the fear of people with the fear of the Lord. Do fear that you might step away from your holy walk with Him. Fear that you are not rightly dividing the Word of God. But never fear or be intimidated by people. There are few missionaries who are willing to speak the truth in love no matter what the cost. Choose this day to be a minister of the gospel who cannot be deterred or intimidated.

In addition, be careful of the contracts you make with people. Some contracts are unconscious ones; we don't even know we're forging an agreement. Some examples:

> *I have to show results (such as conversion numbers) to my partnership team.*

> *As long as you are loyal to me, I will be loyal to you.*

Such relational contracts will compromise your call and must be avoided at all costs. In the end, the only agreements a missionary should make in ministry are to follow Jesus by the power of the Holy Spirit, to love each person with the love of Christ and to speak the truth in love.

Money

Detach from being controlled by money in any way. Of course, you need to make a living. But will you be a slave to the monthly wire to your bank account? Missionaries, which will influence you more: your churches and supporters or the Word of God? Disconnect yourself from the idea that your ministry is a job. Silence the lies that say, "I have to work 80-100 hours per week because I'm living on other people's money." Or "I have to live in poverty, cutting corners to the detriment of my own health." You are employed by a mission organization and faithful partners invest in His work, but you are called by God. Your financial partners do not own you.

Disconnect yourself from the idea that your ministry is a job.

This is a key distinction that must be grounded in the very

foundation of your heart. There will be times in your ministry when people with means will attempt to impose their influence on you. In subtle and not so subtle ways, they will let you know that if you don't agree with them, they will move their support to another missionary.

Longstanding Alliances

Missionary, a person who is presently one of your strongest and healthiest allies may one day not be a part of your team or your company. Believe me, it doesn't take much for such a shift to happen. Detach from the expectation that this person or that person will never leave. Pray this: "Lord, I am thankful for the wonderful co-workers I have. Help me build healthy and true partnerships for Your Kingdom. But my loyalty is to You and to You alone. Though none go with me, still I will follow—no turning back, no turning back."

Criticism

In your ministry, you will discover marvelous and wondrous ways of disappointing people—by being too contextualized (or not contextualized enough), by being too flexible (or too structured) and by investing too much in your team (or not investing enough). Face this truth right now: You are not going to measure up in this or that person's book. Be more concerned about how you're measuring up in God's book!

Detach from the idea that every need is a call.

Someone will not like how you choose to raise your kids, the way you worship or the way you pray. Others will comment regularly on your ministry approach. Detach the tether that causes you to take criticism personally.

As trees and rocks are part of the forest terrain, so is criticism part of the ministry terrain. It is always going to be part of the scenery. Do your best. Share the gospel. Keep listening; keep growing and learning. You'll be fine. Just don't expect everyone to be in the cheering section.

Dedicating Time and Resources

With thousands, even millions within the people group of your focus, where do you commit your time? Detach from the idea that every need is a call. Pray that God would connect you to "people of peace" (Luke 10:6).

As you adjust to varying concepts of time and allow yourself to be stretched in this arena, I encourage you to also keep in mind that some people are addicted to crisis. They want relief but are not willing to do the work required for transformative change. There are families I have worked with for years, dedicating hours and sometimes days to assist them, pray for them, care for them, go to bat for them, cry with them, stand with them. All the while, I was serving them as unto the Lord. I was counting on the thought that, *If we can just get over this hurdle, the family will begin to thrive.*

> *In Christ, you are an environment-changer.*

In almost every situation where a family seemed to require an inordinate amount of effort and ministry time, all my giving seemed to have little or no effect. As a matter of fact, most of these families became resentful that more of my time and resources weren't being allocated to them. Some families are takers. They are not bad people; they simply have no sense of boundaries and are blind to their sense of entitlement. If we relate to people according to their entitlements, our words of truth will be swept away by the tsunami waves of our co-dependent actions.

Moving Forward

Are there more tethers in ministry? Of course! Attachments involving loyalty, success and failure, appearance—these are really just a few. We can find ourselves inadvertently tethered to almost anything.

As our script tethers are detached, we begin to manifest our true calling as ambassadors of our Lord's message and lifestyle. We are called to extend the Kingdom of God wherever we go—in our homes, on the streets, in the lion's den, in our visa platform, in team meetings. He has called us to be His witnesses both locally and globally—even when our new "local" is as far-flung from home as we could imagine. What He has called us to do can be accomplished through the power of His Spirit.

Remember who you are. In Christ, you are an environment-changer. A fully surrendered believer carries tremendous authority in the spiritual realm. David's mighty men accomplished powerful feats for God's glory. Josheb-Basshebeth "raised his spear against eight hundred men, whom he killed in one encounter" (2 Samuel 23:8). Eleazar "stood his ground and struck down the Philistines till his hand grew tired and froze to the sword" (2 Samuel 23:9). Shammah "took his stand in the middle of the field and struck the Philistines down" (2 Samuel 23:12). Even greater power than what these mighty men experienced is available to you through the Spirit of God.

The Psalmist speaks of not fearing "the tens of thousands drawn up against me on every side" (Psalm 3:6). You and I can stand against thousands in the name of Jesus, but first, we must stand victoriously against the natural power of the mirror and the script.

Do the inner work. Tap into His power. Discover who you are in Christ and fulfill your destiny as a powerful warrior of the Most High God!

CHAPTER 2 STUDY QUESTIONS

1. Ministry with PI is definitely in "wild" places. The author quotes Kermit Roosevelt as saying: "When men are off in the wilds . . . they show themselves as they really are. . . and [they] are not always attractive" (p. 23). What do you look like, spiritually and emotionally, under the glaring sun of your ministry life? What do your teammates see? Ask some of them.

2. Ask the Father to let you see yourself through his eyes in Jesus. How does his view of who you really are differ from your own warped view of yourself?

3. What is your default "script" (p. 27) for surviving loss? For surviving disappointment? For surviving criticism? For surviving loneliness? Ask your teammates to pray with you that Jesus will come to you with his power. He already survived all of these things for you.

4. How are you tied to your team's opinion of you? Your sending church's opinion? Your support team's opinion? PI leadership's opinion? Cut those tethers, naming them specifically and aloud. Ask the Father to tie you to Jesus' reputation by the more powerful bonds of the Holy Spirit.

The weapons we fight with are not the weapons of the world. On the contrary, they have divine power to demolish strongholds. We demolish arguments and every pretension that sets itself up against the knowledge of God, and we take captive every thought to make it obedient to Christ. — *2 Corinthians 10:4-5*

CHAPTER 3

KNOW YOUR ENEMY

There are two equal and opposite errors into which our race
can fall about devils. One is to disbelieve in their existence.
The other is to believe, and to feel an excessive and unhealthy
interest in them. They themselves are equally pleased by
both errors, and hail a materialist or a magician with the
same delight.

— C. S. Lewis[7]

On the road that leads from "walking in the flesh" to "walking
in the Spirit," the evil one brings his strongest opposition. He
works to keep you earthbound and weak. And you may well
imagine that he wants no soul to find its way on this path of
life, where you no longer rely on your own understanding.
Therefore, he wants to turn you back from this way of true
ascendancy and strength in God alone.

— John of the Cross[8]

"Look to the Lord," some will say. "Resist the devil" is
also Scripture and I found it worked! ...I found that I
could have victory in the spiritual realm whenever I
wanted it. The Lord Himself resisted the devil vocally:
"Get thee behind me, Satan!" I, in humble dependence
on Him, did the same. I talked to Satan at that time, using the
promises of Scripture as weapons. And they worked. Right
then, the terrible oppression began to pass away.

— James O. Fraser, missionary to China

*Therefore put on the full armor of God, so that when the day
of evil comes, you may be able to stand your ground, and after
you have done everything, to stand.*

— *Ephesians 6:13*

Who is your enemy? It is not the person who slanders
you. It is not the person who is persecuting you or the
neighbors who wish for your demise. The enemy we
struggle against is not "flesh and blood" (Ephesians 6:12); he
is spiritual and more evil than we can imagine. Satan, the
devil, "prowls around like a roaring lion looking for someone to devour" (1 Peter 5:8). He hates the name of Jesus and
labors to veil the glory of Christ by "blinding the minds of
unbelievers so that they cannot see the light of the gospel"
(2 Corinthians 4:4).

Why is he attacking you? You are a child of God. If someone
really wants to hurt me, that person will attack my children.
Satan desires to take as many people to hell with him as he
can. Every child of the King that he captures and kills brings
pain to the very heart of our heavenly Father.

*Why is he attack-
ing you? You are
a child of God.* In his famous work, *The Art of War*, Sun
Tsu writes: "One who knows the enemy
and knows himself will not be in danger
in a hundred battles. One who does not
know the enemy but knows himself will
sometimes win, sometimes lose. One who does not know the
enemy and does not know himself will be in danger in every
battle." No competent commanding officer would lead his or
her troops into battle without first attaining proper intelligence
concerning the assets and vulnerabilities of the opposing army.
In like manner, you must become cognizant of the cunning
strategies of your adversary in order to survive in ministry.

Some of these strategies—such as weariness, discouragement
and isolation—are so subtle that you may assume there is
no supernatural component involved at all. I have come
to believe that the enemy will use any circumstance to his

advantage and our destruction (even circumstances that he did not create).

Therefore, do not be casual concerning this battlefield: Spiritual warfare is an on-going, daily reality for every missionary. Your adversary (along with his army of fallen angels) never gets tired, does not fight fairly and is set upon your destruction. Keep your eyes on the Lord, but also be aware of the following strategies of your adversary.

Weariness

I have discovered that much of the enemy's plan to destroy us has to do with wearing us down and wearing us out. Satan believes he can outlast us. He believes that eventually we will give up. Be aware of this strategy. Take time to rest!

Realize that the terrain changes quickly in ministry. One week, it feels like the world is falling in on you; it feels like things couldn't get worse. Don't react, attack or retreat. Just stand! Stand in faith. These moments of difficulty will pass in due time. It is important that you see that God is able to sustain you in the midst of trials. The next week everything seems to be going well. Be thankful, but realize that there will be challenging days ahead. Don't give yourself to opinions, emotions, or circumstances. Move in the Spirit. Stay on the trail. Keep running the race.

Realize that the terrain changes quickly in ministry.

The missionary life is not a sprint; it is a marathon.

Did you have a tough day? Get some space. Take a nap. Take a walk. Listen to some music. Don't overreact to the day. Rather, respond by the Spirit. Instead of reacting to the daily fluctuations of the "spiritual stock exchange," choose to be a long-term investor in the Word of God. If you remain faithful, your ministry will reap eternal dividends.

The enemy loves to place a large map of the Sahara Desert

in front of your face and remind you how difficult your journey is going to be. As you look at the many challenges set before you, a demon whispers in your ear, "Even if you make it through this day, look how far you still have to go. It is going to take you weeks, months, even decades to get across this desert and you are thirsty already. Give up now! Turn around! Go back to Egypt!" Discouragement is a powerful weapon. The enemy wants you to become overwhelmed and to give up the ground you've worked so hard to gain.

The enemy wants you to become overwhelmed and to give up the ground you've worked so hard to gain.

Refuse to look at the enemy's maps. Reject the lies that you just can't make it, and that you are in a battle you just can't win. Remember the Lord's words: "Do not worry about tomorrow… each day has enough trouble of its own" (Matthew 6:34). When you are weary, don't think too much or talk too much. Don't even glance at the big map when you're tired. Set your sites on getting to the next shelter where you can rest.

By the way, this is the good news that your adversary conveniently forgets to share: There is a shelter waiting for you. There is a place of safety, a strong tower, a place of refreshment and repair. God Himself longs to be your oasis in the desert. In times of weariness, He is more than able to minister to you and give you living water to drink.

Look around you. Thousands of cross-cultural workers are suffering under the desert sun. They find themselves unexpectedly in this unforgiving environment and do not know how to find the Oasis. You, however, must become accustomed to the wilderness regions. You must learn how to wait out the mid-day sun. In the desert, a camel is preferable to the finest thoroughbred horse. Learn from the camel; discover how to survive in the hot sand and the burning heat.

Thank God in the midst of your weariness, for there are lessons that can only be learned in the wilderness. It is there that you discover how God tenderly ministers and gives you victory in this battle. In these seasons, you learn about thirst and the power of living water.

Distancing

Another of Satan's great strategies is to interrupt your intimacy with God and create distance between you and your Lord. He knows that every step you take away from Christ makes you more vulnerable for attack. If you move away from dependency upon Jesus just an inch or two every day, you may lose sight of Him altogether in a couple of weeks.

The enemy wants you to be anywhere except right beside the Lord.

When you were walking right beside the Lord, you felt His breath upon your neck and sensed His gentle promptings throughout the day. From a distance, His voice isn't as clear. You've begun to trust your own understanding and view things from your own perspective. Inch by inch, the enemy has lured you away. Instead of your relationship with the Lord being the priority of your heart, other things—ministry, people and responsibilities—now occupy the center. The sanctuary of your heart has become a marketplace of busyness. The shift is subtle, but don't be fooled. Luring you away from God is a potent strategy of the enemy. From the outside it seems as if your life hasn't changed, but inside your heart has gown cold and your faith stale. This is a frightening spiritual condition. You arrive at that place by moving away from Christ just a little every day.

When you are walking by the Spirit, the enemy has no hope for victory. But separation from God provides the enemy with the leverage he needs to destroy you. Don't give him an inch. Stay close with your Lord.

The enemy wants you to be anywhere except right beside the Lord. He is fine with you lagging behind Jesus. He is equally satisfied if you run ahead. So keep your eyes on your Lord; don't venture out on your own.

Isolation

Do you have people praying for you? Do you have people in your life who know you? Just as a pack of wild dogs looks for the isolated wildebeest, the powers of darkness are searching for missionaries who have separated themselves from their co-workers and support structures. When you are isolated and running on your own, you are vulnerable. Believe me, the wild dogs are watching you all the time and waiting for just the right time to attack. Pull back from the front lines when you need to rest, but don't pull away from your accountability, your prayer coverage, and fellowship with your closest companions. Don't venture out in the field alone; the enemy will be on you in no time.

The Fiery Dart

A fiery dart is a demonically charged weapon strategically aimed at a vulnerable domain of your life and ministry. If your shield of faith does not block it, it can do great damage. Such an attack can come at any time and at any place: at a party, at a prayer gathering, among friends, in the middle of a team meeting, in the midst of casual conversation with local friends. The symptoms vary. It may become difficult for you to think clearly or even to articulate what you are feeling, but you sense that something has invaded you deeply, to the core of your being.

A fiery dart attacks a person's identity and destiny. It is often coated with lies about one's personal worth and value. When you have been pierced in this way, seek the Lord to discover what lies have been introduced into your heart. Confess, repent and take back ground in the name of Christ. Declare the promises of God that directly refute those lies. Remove the dart and ask your close confidants to pray over you for healing.

The All-Out Assault

In addition to the more subtle, cunning, individual threats mentioned above, there will be times when the enemy attacks you from every side. You will be overwhelmed and will experience feelings of resignation, hopelessness and fear. Often, these brutal attacks take place immediately after spiritual victories.

I cannot describe how important it is for you to reach out for your Father's hand when these attacks come upon you. When you are under a full assault, your only shelter is to hide in the "cleft of the rock." Only here will you find power to stand even in the hurricane, as you simply cling to Jesus.

These all-out assaults last for a time, but they *will* pass. Remember this when they come. Every cross-cultural missionary must learn to walk through these vicious storms. No matter what you feel in the moment, if you cling to Jesus, you will emerge victorious.

Moving Forward

Casual mindsets about the strategies and traps of the enemy have led many missionaries to the brink of destruction. Remember this: Every hour of every day, the adversary is seeking to destroy you. His strategic attacks may come at anytime and anywhere—in your thoughts and feelings, in your relationships, in your home, in your office—throughout your life and ministry.

Victory resides in the principles of confession, repentance and complete surrender to Jesus.

Therefore, work to become competent in the domain of spiritual warfare. Study and find yourself approved in this strategic area of ministry. The key to victory resides in the principles of confession, repentance and complete surrender to Jesus. Remember who lives inside you. The enemy is powerful, but the Holy Spirit is exponentially greater. Satan has no ground to defeat us except through our ignorance, fear and disobedience. Walk in the authority that was purchased for every believer through the cross of Christ and, with a mature eye and a fearless heart, take your place in the fight for the release of captives in the name of Jesus!

CHAPTER 3 STUDY QUESTIONS

1. The author notes that "weariness," "discourage-ment" and "isolation" are some of the subtle strate-gies the enemy uses to beat us in battle (p. 36). They are subtle because they seem so mundane that they couldn't have anything to do with spiritual warfare. Ask God to reveal to you some life areas in which you haven't been fighting because you haven't seen them as battlegrounds. Write a prayer committing yourself to put on God's armor in these specific areas of your life.

2. Our enemy doesn't fight fair; he exploits our natural, unavoidable weaknesses. What physical, emotional, or life-experience weaknesses do you (or your family members) have that the enemy turns against you? What would happen if you embraced these same weaknesses as the exact points where the Holy Spirit's power will explode from your life to establish the Father's kingdom?

3. Ask your team to help you discern where the enemy is interrupting your intimacy with God. What "inches" of your life's ground have you given up without even noticing the loss (p. 39)?

4. How competent are you in spiritual warfare? Are you ready to learn? Are you willing to believe that Jesus' authority is yours to fight with? Who (in person or in communication from afar) will the Holy Spirit use to teach you to fight with his weapons?

*Praise be to the Lord, Who has not let us be torn by their teeth.
We have escaped like a bird from the fowler's snare; the snare
has been broken, and we have escaped.* — *Psalm 124:6-7*

CHAPTER 4

KNOW THE TERRAIN

In a free country, to be a member of a church, it is enough to believe and to be baptized. In the Church underground it is not enough to be a member in it. You can be baptized and you can believe, but you will not be a member of an underground church unless you know how to suffer. You might have the mightiest faith in the world, but if you are not prepared to suffer, then you will be taken by the police. You will get two slaps and you will declare anything. So the preparation for suffering is one of the essentials of the preparation of underground work.

— Richard Wurmbrand, founder of Voice of the Martyrs[9]

There was a time in my life when I went through intense trials such as I had never faced before. I became rude and harsh with those closest to me. I cried out to the Lord, "Where is all this anger coming from? It wasn't here before!"

The Lord responded, "Son, it is when they liquefy gold in fire that the impurities show up." He then asked a question that changed my life. "Can you see the impurities in gold before it is put in the fire?"

"No," I answered.

"But that doesn't mean they were not there," He said. "When the fire of trials hit you, these impurities surfaced. Though hidden to you, they were always visible to Me. So now you have a choice that will determine your future. You can remain angry, blaming your wife, friends, pastor and the people you work with, or you can see this dross of sin for what it is and repent, receive forgiveness, and I will take My ladle and remove these impurities from your life."

— John Bevere, evangelist and Bible teacher[10]

The terrain of ministry is full of life-giving opportunities. It is also full of snares. Become a student of the ground upon which your ministry will either rise or fall. You must have open and seeing eyes. Take notice of both the high places that offer advantage and the valleys that make you vulnerable. Decide now to become a student of the terrain. Be alert and aware; your life depends on it.

The Holy Spirit desires for us to be "wise as serpents and innocent as doves" (Matthew 10:16). Our enemy is setting traps and snares throughout the wilderness in order to destroy us. We must train ourselves to see what others don't normally see. What looks safe at first glance may not be safe. A good trap is hidden from sight. A good snare entices its prey with attractive bait. We cannot afford to be fooled.

Pits

Watch your step; watch your heart! There are deep pits all around you. These cavernous and cold places have names like "anger," "resentment" and "bitterness." They exist throughout the terrain of ministry and pose a very real danger.

Understand that you *will* encounter mistreatment and various forms of persecution as you minister in the name of Christ. Such attacks—and remember that we battle not against flesh and blood—will strike at the very core of your personhood and identity. There will be times when you are misrepresented and slandered by brothers and sisters whom you've walked with for years. Others will believe lies about you. At times, you will become angry and full of pain. Don't strike back. Realize that your emotions will blind you

There will be times when you are misrepresented and slandered.

48

from seeing clearly. Before you know it, you can be swallowed up in those deep pits.

Survival Tactic:

If you have fallen into one of these pits, there are ways to escape and recover. God can provide spiritual ropes and ladders through His grace and through the community of faith. However, as with all weaknesses and snares, it is far better to avoid them altogether.

To do this, you must learn how not to allow your emotional pain governance over your actions. Max Lucado refers to this danger when he writes, "Linger too long in the stench of your hurt, and you'll smell like the toxin you despise."[11] Many missionaries have fallen into a pit of anger and resentment, and some never recover. To avoid this, I encourage you to have the conversations that are necessary, and then forgive and release people. Christian author and poet George Herbert articulated it well when he said, "He who cannot forgive another, breaks the bridge over which he must pass himself."

Many missionaries have fallen into a pit of anger and resentment.

Carnal Temptations

As fourth-century philosopher Mencius said, "Before a man can do things there must be things he will not do." No one is exempt from having to battle the time-tested carnal temptations of the flesh and the world.

Do not underestimate the power of lust. Every missionary knows that "the cravings of sinful man, the lust of his eyes and the boasting of what he has and does comes not from the Father but from the world" (1 John 2:16). Nonetheless, many thousands have fallen into the miry clay of pornography, fantasy and lewdness of all kinds. It is important to note that lust includes a craving for illicit intimacy—an emotional affair and/or deep companionship with a person that crosses healthy boundaries. In these cases, we are being lured into satisfying our God-given desires (to be loved, to be known, to be affirmed, to be comforted, etc.) in an ungodly way.

The world unashamedly promotes sensuality: on the Internet, on the streets, on television. It is so accessible and attractive to the carnal nature, but hidden beneath the bait is a deadly hook. Satan is a fisherman of souls, and lust is one of his shiniest lures.

Survival Tactic:

Establish accountability with two or three missionaries (of your own gender and preferably not on your team) concerning your thought life and struggle with any unholy patterns. Connect regularly with this group and pray for one another.

In these moments you must choose Jesus over sin.

Be on alert at all times, but especially when you are under stress. It is in those moments that you will crave comfort and immediate satisfaction. Your enemy will place a shiny lure right before your eyes when you are most hungry for a hug.

In addition, strengthen your self-control by abstaining from different things. Abstain from sugar, television or (forbid the thought) even coffee for a time—if only to exercise your ability to combat the craving for comfort. Learn to say "no" to immediate gratification. Apply the Apostle Paul's testimony to yourself: "I beat my body and make it my slave, so that after I have preached to others, I myself will not be disqualified for the prize" (1 Corinthians 9:27).

In these moments you must choose Jesus over sin. If you train for the battle daily, you will be able to hold out and hold on when temptation comes knocking. It is true: You can be victorious only in *His* strength. However, you must use *your* willpower to choose His strength. Develop the muscles of your will by practicing the discipline of saying "no" to yourself.

Keep watch. Someone is fishing for your soul every minute of every day and every night. There is a hook, a terrible hook, hidden in the bait.

Stress-filled Moments and Settings

Most missionaries are able to extend grace and offer kindness to others when life is going well, but how do you relate when life becomes stressful? How do you respond to people when you are hungry, tired or overwhelmed by the culture around you? Ministry is full of surprises. Sudden changes and unanticipated challenges will meet you almost every day. I've seen talented missionaries discredit themselves in a few short, pressurized moments by their reaction to a stressful time. It wasn't just the moment that destroyed them, but the lack of preparation leading up to it. People are watching! Your demeanor in the midst of trials will make or break your testimony.

> *Choose to walk in the power of God and be an instrument of His peace, grace and love.*

Survival Tactic:

Learn how to feed off stress-filled circumstances instead of those circumstances feeding off of you! When the whole room is filled with anxiety, be the one who is able to remain peaceful. When the whole team loses hope, be the one who reclaims it. When others lash out, be the one who does not react out of the flesh. When others resign, be the one who continues to stand.

In order to walk by the Spirit when circumstances become challenging, you must have eyes to see what is happening in the spiritual realm. Observe and learn. Recognize that the Lord has brought you to this stress-filled environment for a reason. He's giving you an opportunity to shine for Him! Don't allow your surroundings to control you. Remember who you are and whose blood runs through your veins. You have but one Master: the Lord Jesus! Therefore, do not bow your knee to circumstances or be conformed to the moment. Choose to walk in the power of God and be an instrument of His peace, grace and love.

People need to see something more than the talking kind of faith in their missionary friends. Everyone performs well on calm and sunny days. A person's true colors become apparent when the storms hit. In stressful moments, in the crucible of the flame, the talking kind of faith becomes exposed and the standing kind of faith is revealed.

Do you want the standing kind of faith? If so, you must observe what happens to your body, mind and spirit when you encounter stress. Learn how you naturally respond when you're hungry, when you're offended, when you're tired. Discover your natural limits and begin to stretch those limits.

Like a professional athlete who learns to perform competently even when injured, so each of us must learn to practice self-control in the midst of difficult circumstances. Go to the edge on your own. Fast a day and pray all night, and then attend your team meeting. Observe yourself. Learn how irritability, distraction and offense are magnified when your body isn't fully content.

Satan will discover any attitude in you that resonates with the spirit of carnality.

Keep alert. Stress can enter into your life anywhere and at anytime. Be careful to keep your head when you're tired, hungry and frustrated. Be aware of stressful moments and seize those opportunities to be an environment-changer.

Sabotage: Turning You Against You

There are sounds—echoes of the past—that have the ability to cause us to cringe in the present. These are emotional echoes or associations that control us.

A river of pain flows through your life. It flows with the tears, hurts and disappointments you've experienced during your years on earth. Whenever you experience fresh pain, the water level and the speed of the current of this river grow.

Satan is a terrorist, and he has plans to make use of your river of pain. His hope is that you will ignore it until it overflows its banks and wreaks havoc in your life and ministry. You must be proactive in dealing with this river of pain before it destroys you. Allow all your injuries, all your disappointments, all your hurts, all your pain and shame to flow to the foot of the cross. If you don't, one day this toxic river will flood your relationships and devastate your ministry.

The same is true of other aspects of your fleshly nature. Are you thirsty for affirmation and approval? The enemy will capitalize on that need. Are you lonely and starving for intimacy? The enemy will introduce an inappropriate avenue of satisfaction. Are you susceptible to pride? Don't be surprised if you are offered a kingdom. Are you insecure? Be sure that the enemy will try to shame you. Satan will discover any attitude in you that resonates with the spirit of carnality, and he will call it to allegiance.

Jesus has called you to serve faithfully. Keep your eye on this task.

Survival Tactic:

Recognize that you may be able to hide your vulnerabilities from people around you, but any sinful attitude or behavior is a giant bull's eye in the spiritual realm. Neutralize all of these by way of confession and pleading the blood of Christ. After that, be sure to put on the belt of truth, because arguments that set themselves up against the knowledge of God (2 Corinthians 10:5) will assuredly be coming your way.

Comparison

Comparing ourselves or our ministries to others is a common and tenacious trap. It is common in that the enemy sets this trap frequently and in many domains of ministry. It is tenacious because once we fall prey to its claws, escape is difficult.

Comparison traps succeed when our eyes shift from a singular focus on Jesus to a roaming focus on other people and other things. The very minute our audience becomes more than One, the vicious claw of this trap is already being sprung.

People will push you into this comparison trap (usually un-intentionally):

"I'm excited about what's happening in your teammate's ministry."

"Another company's ministry in your city is thriving."

"My previous team leader was someone who just loved people."

Survival Tactic:

Jesus has called you to serve faithfully. Keep your eye on this task. Be thankful for the others who have embraced the wilderness of cross-cultural ministry. If their ministries seem to be flourishing more than yours, so be it. God sees each part of the mission field and is watching how you plow, plant, water or harvest in your area of responsibility. Take your cues from Him and Him alone.

These are sins that have somehow become permissible within the Body of Christ.

Get this straight in your heart and fix your eyes upon Jesus. There will always be someone who is smarter, quicker, wittier, more gifted than you. There will always be missionaries who are better students of culture or who seem to have more energy than you. Stop the madness that comes from comparing. Be yourself. Do not evaluate your success by looking at others. Be faithful in your call and rejoice that you are working with others all around the world for the cause of Christ!

Sleeping Potion

Something as obvious as swallowing a sleeping potion may seem like a small risk, but have you ever succumbed to the thought, "I'll just rest my eyes here for a few minutes..."? Before you know it, years have passed by and nothing has changed. "A little sleep, a little slumber, a little folding of the hands to rest—and poverty will come on you like a bandit and scarcity like an armed man" (Proverbs 6:10-11).

Survival Tactic:

Do not fall asleep! Keep awake and alert! When you move in the power of the Holy Spirit, there will be an edge to your life. Keep that edge. Don't become casual. Rest only in safe places and when you know someone else is keeping watch on the wall.

Toxins

Complaining and Spirit-quenching are like toxins in mission endeavors. They will prevent growth. There are people who you may be called to work with who insist on tearing apart the team strategy, speaking about teammates behind their backs and finding fault in ideas even before they get off the ground.

Complainers are relentless. They have lost the ability to be content in all situations and thankful in everything. These are sins that have somehow become permissible within the Body of Christ, even though they are terribly destructive. They quench, sour and choke the sense of community within your team, let alone your witness among the people group you serve. If you allow it, this negativity will also take its toll on you, filling you with discouragement and hopelessness.

Once the free flow of toxins has ceased, the air will begin to clear.

Other spiritual toxins include discouragement, fear, depression, gossip, slander and anxiety. Some poisons (like discouragement and depression) might require prolonged exposure or repeated ingestion to shut down a ministry. Some (like fear, gossip and slander) are potent, quickly attacking the neurological system of a ministry, causing paralysis or even death.

Survival Tactic:

Work with your team and ministry to create a "fresh air" environment where young plants can flourish. Imagine planting a garden and then allowing someone to spray poison on your plants. Sour faces, sour glances and sour words are like poison.

They often come from those who have lost their first love and resent others who still have some measure of passion and faith.

Eradicate complaining, gossip and judgment within your team. Stand against these sins that kill "first love" worship and "first love" life! Stand guard at the gate of your garden. Teach people that complaining is not Christ-like behavior and that extending grace is.

Imagine laughing at a five-year-old trying to learn how to read; she might get discouraged and give up on learning. In the same way, it is wrong to complain when someone on your team doesn't get things perfectly while exercising his gift. There is a place for loving correction; there is no place for complaining or hurtful criticism. Create an environment of learning and acceptance wherein people will be encouraged to step out of the boat and try walking on water.

Let your team see your vigilance in this regard. Follow the Matthew 18 model of correcting mishaps and immature behavior. Sloppy ministry is not our best testimony to the world. Correct laziness and press toward excellence, but save your rebukes for the complainer. Regardless of whether you're a team leader or a team member, set the standard concerning complaining or gossip. Permit it no longer! As your team begins to clean out the toxins, you will discover that you've made some enemies in the camp. Complainers are prideful people. Do not be surprised if some people decide to leave your team if they can't "be themselves" and "give their opinion about everything." In spite of this, press on in this regard. Negativity must die in the name of Jesus.

Friendly fire is a real and present danger in every ministry context.

Once the free flow of toxins has ceased, the air will begin to clear in team meetings. A new freedom, a new gentleness, a new excitement will begin to emerge. What has happened in the spiritual realm? People who were once afraid to find their voice and share their gifts are now stepping forward.

The Holy Spirit has now been given room to minister through His body.

The antidotes for all spiritual toxins are the blood of the Lamb, obedience to the Word of God and the choice to walk by faith not by sight. Be prepared for chemical attacks and keep the air on your team fresh and holy.

The Minefield of Relationships

Perhaps the phrase "minefield of relationships" seems pessimistic, an exaggeration of the danger. But I believe that this realm is the most treacherous terrain that you will face in your career. There is a tendency for missionaries to look outside the camp for attacks, but friendly fire is a real and present danger in every ministry context.

God desires missionaries to establish and enjoy healthy relationships. And what God desires for us can be accomplished. But relationships are complex, and the minefield we must cross has real explosives.

Survival Tactic:

A minefield can be crossed with proper equipment. It is a matter of knowing where the explosives are. The One who clears the path of danger will show you precisely where to place your feet. Jesus will guide you on this journey. Let me give you some examples of the explosives in the field of relationships.

Loyalty

Fallacy: "If you love me and respect me, you will have my back no matter what the circumstance. You will keep my secrets, even if the secrets are not healthy ones."

Be loyal to people for the sake of the Kingdom, but not for the sake of the relationship. Reverence communication, but do not be a secret-keeper. Healthy relationships welcome truth and honesty. Healthy relationships are not co-dependent and hidden.

Keep a sharp eye out for loyalty issues. They are often invisible (unconscious and unseen in the relationship) but very strong.

Ledger

Fallacies: "You owe me. I took care of you in the past—and now I'm calling in a favor."

"You made a mistake and I forgave you. But it was a bad mistake and you are still indebted to me."

Healthy relationships have a balanced ledger; one party doesn't "owe" the other party an extraordinary amount of emotional currency. Keep your accounts clean. If you are indebted to someone, work hard to pay back the debt in a healthy way. Do not be blackmailed or manipulated by the ledger. If you can be manipulated or bought, you have lost your moral authority.

Moving Forward

Avoid the dangers I have mentioned above, but also be proactive by looking to the terrain-changing tools of prayer, worship and equipping (detailed in Chapter 6) in order to create acres and acres of fruit-producing saints for the Kingdom of God.

CHAPTER 4 STUDY QUESTIONS

1. Draw a picture of your current terrain. What surrounds you now and what lies ahead? Share your picture with your team, noting what snares and pitfalls are most dangerous for you at this time.

2. Review the survival tactics described in this chapter. In light of the picture you drew, which tactic(s) do you need to prioritize this month? Share with one other person the steps you will take to make this a reality.

3. How are the muscles of your will doing? Tell your team about one area in which you'd like to strengthen this God-given resource.

4. What stresses in your adopted culture influence you the most? How can you as a team work to capitalize on these stresses?

But Jesus would not entrust himself to them, for he knew all people. He did not need human testimony about them, for he knew what was in them. —John 2:24-25

CHAPTER 5

KNOW YOUR BOUNDARIES

In the States, if you are not busy, you do not have a life. So going from fast paced, scheduled days to a culture that is so laid back that their motto is rubber time, you could find yourself going a little crazy. The months leading up to leaving the country, our schedule was nonstop on the go. In our new country we realized that our calendar was empty for days, weeks and months to come. Our job now was to adapt to this culture–that was it. But what do you do when you don't think you're doing enough, because in the States everything was go, go, go? What do you do when going to language school wears you out and you can't do anymore? It's a hard lesson to learn, living life one day at a time and not moving 100 miles per hour.

— a missionary in Southeast Asia

During our early years, we hosted most team meetings in our home. The scurry to get the house in order, have some goodies ready, set up the rooms for sleeping babies and the ensuing late night contributed to an overwhelming sense that we were leaving our children in the lurch. In an effort to make clear to them that they were still a central concern for me, I endeavored to keep the bedtime story-reading tradition going, even when guests were in the home. Sometimes this meant that our guests would be left sitting in our living room for up to 30 minutes while we disappeared to give bedtime its proper ceremony. I found myself hurrying through these moments with a vague sense of guilt hanging over my head.

Years later, an ex-teammate approached me to thank me for those minutes of abandonment in our living room. "You gave me permission to take care of my children too. Thank you for modeling that." My only regret is that I did not fully enter into that time with my children due to the rushed guilt feelings. Now I know better.

— a missionary in East Asia

My life of service to God had always exemplified responsibility, commitment, passion for education and professionalism. My marriage was what I considered healthy and strong. We seemed to be a model "poster family" for missions...I never would have imagined before leaving for the field that I would have succumbed to the temptation of having an emotional affair. It was a total surprise that this could have happened to me, but I found that no one is exempt. Everyone has the potential to fall if the circumstances are right.

— a missionary in India

I had a difficult conversation several years ago with a friend in the ministry who had fallen because of adultery. I asked, "What in the world were you doing? Didn't you hear the alarm bells going off?"

There was a long silence, then the man answered, "Oh Bob, I did hear the alarms. I heard the alarms plainly. But when I heard the alarms I decided to disconnect the wires."

— Dr. Bob Reccord, speaker and author[12]

In His earthly ministry, Jesus never turned anyone away. At the same time, He did not allow everyone to have complete access to Him. He disclosed Himself most fully to His Father. Then, at differing levels, He disclosed His heart to the three, the twelve, the seventy and the multitudes.

We are not called to be independent or co-dependent, but inter-dependent with other believers. We are called to community, but what does this mean? How closely are we to travel together?

Your survival will depend in part on how you answer these

questions and, more specifically, on your ability to establish and respect healthy boundaries. Boundaries are walls, fences, doors and gates—not simply in the physical realm, but in the emotional, relational and spiritual realms as well.

Consider the doors of your home. Are they propped open at all hours of the day or do you close and even lock them at various times? In the same way, you must stand watch and attend to your emotional and spiritual doors, especially in the following domains.

Boundaries of Time and Schedule

Balancing family and ministry commitments is a challenge in any location, but add to that the cross-cultural dimension of adapting to your host culture and the situation is complex. Keeping appropriate boundaries in your passport culture is hard enough, but what do they look like in Asia or the Middle East? How do you juggle language study, the business that secures your visa, church-planting work and time with your family? Learn to pray frequently, "God, what are the appropriate boundaries *here*?" Where possible, find someone who's been in the culture longer than you have and ask for his or her advice.

Keeping appropriate boundaries in your passport culture is hard enough, but what do they look like in Asia or the Middle East?

One non-negotiable is Sabbath-keeping. A missionary in Central Asia says, "My staff knows that I 'go to America' every Thursday. I don't speak Dari, I don't entertain and I don't work." It's her weekly day of rest. Be ruthless about keeping these. Fight for them or you will not make it. Keeping a Sabbath is part of the Ten Commandments for a reason.

I like R.C. Steven's reflections from South Asia on ministry and rest:

First, there will always be need. In fact, there will always be more need than we are able to meet—even if we work night and day and don't stop to eat. Every time I walk out my door I am faced with more need than I can ever meet in my entire lifetime. Some days this makes me want to retreat back inside and bar the door. But it shouldn't. It should simply help me realize my own limitations and remind me not to try to be God.

Second, very often, Christian workers try to be God anyway. Meeting needs is not a bad thing. After all, God has also commissioned us to preach and heal and cast out demons. In short, we are called to meet needs—just not every need. Only God can do that. Unfortunately, we often get so busy meeting so many needs that we become needy ourselves! I can't think of anyone who couldn't use a good vacation. In extreme cases people leave and don't return. Burnout, brownout, emotional fatigue—whatever we call it—the remedy is the same. And so, we need every bit as much as the disciples to hear Jesus say:

"Come with me by yourselves to a quiet place and get some rest."

It is greatly encouraging to me to hear Jesus utter these words. He understands our need for rest. He doesn't expect us to continue on indefinitely—not having time to eat, to grieve or to celebrate. He deliberately calls us aside to be with Himself and find rest.

Guard Your Family

We've all heard the nightmare story about the missionary every local person loves. "He's always there for us—so caring, so wise, so gentle and kind!" But his wife is bitter towards him. She feels abandoned. He's always on call. Even when he's home he's not really home. His children have rejected the faith. This missionary has had an affair with his work, and the family hates him for it.

Learn from the thousands of shipwrecked missionaries who have gone before you. If you are married, create a rigid boundary around family times. Your family relationships comprise a significant part of your calling on this earth. Your spouse and children need to be with you and you need to be with them. Chart the flow of your week, your spouse's week and your children's week, and then choose to be present with your family at agreed upon times. Time at home is not simply time out of the office. You must be present. Turn the cell phone off; don't look at your e-mails. As much as is in your power, don't let your mind wander to issues of your ministry. (Rest assured that they will be waiting for you tomorrow in all their glory.)

The main point is this: Missions can easily consume every moment of your time and every ounce of your energy. If you don't set boundaries, you won't

> *God created us to live a balanced life.*

have a healthy marriage, a healthy family or any real friendships. If this happens, you are in great danger of becoming a very strange and unlovely animal: the non-human, functional missionary on his or her way to burning out. I can tell you with certainty that this is not God's design for any missionary. Therefore, create boundaries for your personal times with the Lord, for your times of study, for building intimacy with your spouse, for parenting your children, for your rest and recreation, for times together as a family and for friends.

God created us to live a balanced life. The Hebrew word *shalom* not only connotes peace and welfare, but also right alignment and balance. The Christian walk can be likened to a balance beam. Speed and strength are admirable traits, but on the beam, balance is the key. Satan does not care what it is that throws us off balance; he simply wants us to fall. A missionary who does not guard personal time and family time will lose balance and fall.

Emotional Boundaries

Whom do you bring into your inner sanctuary? To whom do you disclose your deeper self, both personally and professionally? Be careful whom you trust. Gather people of character and maturity around you—even if it can only be virtually through e-mail.

Gender

Survey statistics from *Men's Secret Wars* indicate that 64 percent of missionaries, pastors or church staff struggle with sexual addiction or compulsion.[13] Twenty-five percent admitted to having sexual intercourse with someone besides their wife while married, even after they had accepted Christ. Another 14 percent admitted some form of sexual contact short of intercourse.

How do you steer clear of being one of these statistics? Begin simply. Men, don't meet alone with women. Women, don't meet alone with men. Create safe structures wherein no one has any ground to accuse you of impropriety. Establish safe and credible accountability when meeting people of the opposite gender so that you do not bring dishonor to your Lord and compromise your ministry career.

The power of emotional touch is more subtle, but equally, if not more, powerful.

In addition, respect the power of physical touch. Some hugs can be good, some can be bad. The power of emotional touch is more subtle, but equally, if not more, powerful. Prayer, counseling and spiritual discussions can be very intimate, and before you know it, an attraction can emerge. Many missionaries who have fallen into sexual affairs can honestly say they had no plans or interest in the physical aspect of the relationship. Their emotional intimacy tank was empty. They were looking for companionship, a caring listener, a trusted confidant. Intimacy, the sharing of dreams and feelings, is a serious drug to the body and to the soul.

It is lovely when someone really listens, when someone truly cares. Emotional connection is like a direct injection of adrenalin into the human heart! Do not underestimate its power. People will come to you depleted of hope and raw with feeling of abandonment and rejection. Your careful listening and authentic concern will seem to them like an oasis in the Sahara. Men, she is so thirsty for your kindness. It is something she just doesn't get from her husband. Women, he is craving the gentle support you are offering. His marriage is cold and he feels alone. Be very careful! Remember: God created us for intimacy. Be aware of your thirst for intimacy and how that thirst is met.

Our culture is obsessed with sex, and people are hungry for love. This is a dangerous combination. Anyone can be tempted and fall into sin. Missionaries who believe they are immune to physical or emotional affairs are self-deceived and are leaving themselves wide open to attack.

If two people don't meet privately, it is difficult for a romantic attraction to develop, but don't be fooled. Phone calls, e-mails and working in ministry together can also create a strong emotional connection. Before you know it, you find yourself "falling in love." In just a few short months you become involved in a relationship that could decimate your ministry call.

> Someone may make it his or her mission to take you down.

Relationally Wounded People

God calls you to love people as He loves them. Be wise as serpents and innocent as doves concerning this high and worthy call on your life. Realize that nearly every person has been wounded deeply in the realm of relationship, particularly in the foundational domain of trust. The giants of abandonment and rejection loom large on the horizon of our lives.

Wounded people will approach you with their emotional baggage. They do not know the extent of the danger that they carry. Beware! Even though most people do not have it in their minds to harm you, take care to protect yourself and others from people with emotional and relational wounds that can act like weapons.

Highly Dangerous People

A final word of warning: At some point in your career, a person or persons you serve alongside may attempt to destroy you and your ministry. Why? The reasons are varied. Sometimes a person will become fully convinced that you are evil (or abusive, or false, or incompetent, etc.) and that you must be stopped in the name of Jesus. Another reason might be retaliation. (The person is attacking you because of an offense or a deep wound he or she has received.) Other possible reasons involve issues of authority/control or acceptance/rejection, or relational close-ness/distance. The turmoil that has been dormant within them for years has now been awakened. Their personal thunderstorm has been unleashed, and you're the one standing in the field holding a lightning rod. Whatever the reasons, I am warning you that this may happen. Someone may make it his or her mission to take you down.

You may be surprised that these particular people have become advocates for your destruction. You would have never guessed that they would be attacking you in this way and with this level of intensity. Their words and actions seem incongruous, out of balance with the act that offended them. A deeper pain within their hearts has been uncovered, and you're the one who's going to get the full assault.

Where possible, limit what you write in letters and e-mails.

In such a case, assess the danger, and then confirm your assessment with your supervisor. Set a rigid boundary between you and those who are attacking you. Never meet alone with them. Never speak on the phone with them without a third party listening in. Always work with a witness at your side. Many missionaries have lost their careers not because they sinned, but because they were careless concerning this boundary.

Boundaries in Communication

E-mails and Written Correspondence

Keep in mind that e-mail is one-way communication. It is quite limiting in any conversation that has to do with relationships. A great deal of communication comes through non-verbal cues such as facial expression, tone of voice, gestures and posture. Clarification and the "give and take" of a conversation cannot be achieved in written correspondence. Yet this is the reality in which you live.

Where possible, limit what you write in letters and e-mails. E-mails will get forwarded. Do not be casual or lax with them.

Save every important e-mail you write or receive. You never know when you will need to give an accounting for your words.

If you are corresponding via e-mail with a person whose relationship with you is complex (for example, it might be intense or conflicted), here are some suggestions regarding a path forward:

1. Write to the person and explain that e-mail communication is limiting and is not the best way to have an important and heart-felt conversation. Let the person know that you are willing to have this discussion face-to-face or by video-enabled Skype, but not via e-mail.

I always want to know who is receiving the communication I am reading.

2. Communicate to the person that having another person present can greatly enhance such a meeting. "Let's design our time together so that we're doing all we can to listen to one another and further the work of Christ."

3. Propose a path forward: "Let's schedule this meeting. If I don't hear from you in a week, I'll be contacting you. Communicating about this is important to me."

For a person who continues to use e-mail inappropriately and won't adhere to the procedure outlined above, respond to their e-mail in the following way: "As I have stated before, I am willing to discuss this in person or via video Skype, but I am not willing to continue this conversation through e-mail. Starting with the next e-mail, all correspondence that I send to you or receive from you will be copied/forwarded to my supervisor so that a third party can help us in this communication."

Some people will resent you for copying e-mails to a third-party, but I have found that it is a necessary practice in this medium of communication. A further note about e-mail: I do not like the "blind copy" feature. I always want to know who is receiving the communication I am reading, so I want to afford the recipients of my e-mails the same courtesy. In this way, you model healthy, straightforward communication within all your relationships.

Phone Conversations

The same principles hold true with phone conversations. Unless you are on a conference call, there is no witness to the conversation you are having. Therefore, do not enter into deep or challenging discussions over the phone. Use the phone to design the proper environment to have the critical discussion.

Confidentiality

Reverence communication, but do not participate in secret-keeping. When someone begins to disclose sensitive information to you ("I did something I'm very ashamed of." Or "I'm planning on taking an action that no one else knows about yet."), interrupt them. Explain that you are willing to listen and help him or her walk with integrity and accomplish the Lord's purposes. In order to accomplish this, you may not be able to keep secret what they are about to disclose. If the information about to be shared causes you to believe the person speaking or someone else might be in danger, then you have an ethical, moral and legal responsibility to intervene and include other people in the discussion.

Otherwise, what will you do when you have vowed to keep a secret and the person tells you they are contemplating suicide? What will you do when the person discloses his or her moral infidelity? Beware, or you will find yourself caught in this communication trap.

Never promise to keep secrets. Be a trustworthy minister of the gospel who serves lovingly and respectfully concerning the brokenness of others, but do not get trapped in the snare of secret-keeping.

Moving Forward

Competence in the area of boundary setting (or the lack of it) can make or break a missionary's career. Whether in the domain of communication, schedule or friendship, be vigilant in guarding the doorways of your life and ministry. Be aware that most people are not cognizant of the subtle principles of healthy boundaries; at times they cross lines inappropriately without even knowing it. When it happens, approach it the same as driving a car defensively; another driver at the intersection might choose to do something crazy, so keep your eyes open. As you maintain biblical boundaries, your team and those you minister to will learn and benefit from your example. Check your doors and gates. Make sure they are functioning properly, so that you can live out your calling in the power of the Spirit!

CHAPTER 5 STUDY QUESTIONS

1. Which boundaries are hardest for you to keep? Why? What's one step you can take this week to remedy this? At your next team meeting, check in with each other about the progress you've made.

2. Look at the "doors and gates" in the lives of your teammates. Take part of a team meeting to affirm at least one good boundary you observe in each person.

3. It's been said, "Not every need is a call." Do you agree? Why or why not? Are there needs that you should let go of meeting in order to fulfill your call?

4. Place this chapter next to the list of PI's core values (passion for God, UPGs, CPMs, the local ch, team centered, innovation & flexibility, ethos of grace, participatory servant leadership). Where do they overlap? Are there any core values in which boundaries need to be strengthened?

I have set you an example that you should do as I have done for you. —John 13:15

CHAPTER 6

KNOW HOW TO LEAD

Paul and Barnabas appointed elders for them in each church and, with prayer and fasting, committed them to the Lord in whom they had put their trust.

— Acts 14:23

Do not be hasty in the laying on of hands...

— 1 Timothy 5:22

Every missionary is a leader. You have chosen to do what few others will do. You've left the familiar for the unknown. Others are called to follow your example. As a result, you are held to a higher standard than most. So whether you hold an official title of "leader" within your company or not, listen in. This chapter is for you.

Power, Authority and Leadership

I've heard it said that where two or three people are gathered together, there is a struggle for power. This is true not only in the secular world, but also within ministries. You must be very aware of power and authority issues within yourself, within others and in the churches you plant.

What should leadership look like? It should be servant-like in attitude (Philippians 2:5-7), plural in form (Titus 1:5, Acts 14:23), mature in character (1 Timothy 3:1-7, Titus 1:5-9), unified in purpose (Philippians 2:2-4), biblical in thinking (2 Timothy 2:15), and courageous in leading (1 Peter 5:1-4). A team must be committed to Kingdom ministry. Decisions should be made by consensus. Every member must have a voice, as well as be a team player (open to correction, not easily offended, teachable) and have only one agenda: To hear from God and obey His direction.

God has called you to minister within community and accountability.

Many missionary teams split apart or shut down due to the misuse of power, poor management style or a lack of team mentality. Do not think for a moment that any missionary is immune to this danger. God has called you to minister within community and accountability. You need a team. Even in your best moments, you have blindness and limited understanding. Gather around you a team that will help model the body of Christ to the unreached peoples you serve.

Qualities of Team Members

I believe that every missionary in pioneering church-planting ministry needs to be held to the standard of an elder. You are commissioned by your church to be an ambassador of the gospel. Are the following traits evident in your life?

- The required character qualities of an elder (1 Timothy 3:1-7; Titus 1:5-9). Take them seriously. Exhibit the "fruit of the Spirit" (Galatians 5:22-23), which can be formed only through constant abiding in Christ. Your teammates will see your true character over time—especially in tense, emotionally-filled situations. You can truly tell what's in the heart of a person when he or she is squeezed.

- A personal relationship with Jesus, a mature theology and a solid knowledge of the Bible. Intimacy with the Lord is essential. A love for the Word is essential. How's your hermeneutic? Do you have a consistent methodology in interpreting Scripture? Do you have a developed systematic theology? These tools are foundational.

- A solid sense of self. You cannot draw your identity from the opinions of others. You must be a principled person of conviction, certain of your identity and destiny in Christ.

- A willingness to mutually submit to other leaders and to be part of a team. It is not possible to overemphasize this point, so please take it to heart. People who are unwilling to hear other perspectives can destroy a team more quickly than anyone else. I'd rather have a witch standing outside the door of our church speaking curses over our ministry than to have a teammate with his or her own agenda. Such members are arrogant, self-righteous and extremely dangerous. A teammate *The faithful coworkers that God has brought around you are your most valuable resource.* who is unwilling to submit to the team and prayerfully consider the counsel of the members can bring destruction to the team as a whole. Missionaries are given spiritual authority as they seek to plant churches. A lack of submission on their part will lead to division and destruction. Practice submission and humility.

- An earnest desire to serve and shepherd the church in an unreached area. Unless you really want to equip and serve people, you are not ready to be a missionary.

- An ability and giftedness to move as an overseer in the church. The gift set required of an overseer includes the ability to listen, to reason and to prayerfully consider various options.

Leadership Development

The real testimony of a mature team is when it continues to thrive even when the team leader is absent. In order for this to occur, members must become vision-bearers, not just vision-repeaters. They must be trailblazers, working together for the Kingdom of God.

Spend time developing and caring for your fellow teammates. Pay close and consistent attention to their needs. The faithful coworkers that God has brought around you are your most valuable resource. For most of my ministry, I was drawn to the "squeaky wheel," or to the sudden "brushfires" breaking out around me. The urgent requires some attention, but caregiving and pouring into those who are faithfully serving became one of my key priorities. The battle is great in the lives of people dedicated to the Lord's work. Do not believe the lie that because a teammate is not complaining he or she does not need prayer or encouragement. Pay close attention to the health of your colleagues. Satan wants nothing more than to destroy the workers and visionaries whom God has placed around you.

Take time to bless, encourage, listen and pray for each leader on your team.

Spend time with your team members on a consistent basis. During part of the time you meet, do not discuss strategy. Rather, focus on each teammate's life and spiritual development. Take time to bless, encourage, listen and pray for each leader on your team.

Invest in team development. Schedule at least one retreat a year. Make it a priority to come alongside each other. Keep your eyes on the relational dynamics of your team. One strategy of the enemy is to divide and conquer. Satan will attempt to isolate a particular member of your team. Be proactive! Don't wait until your team is broken beyond repair. Be courageous to address avoidance, disconnection, relational distance or resentments. In so doing, you establish a line of defense for your team, thus protecting it from the enemy's primary plan of attack.

Multiplication of Ministry

As you reach out to the people you are called to serve, mentor those who will someday mentor others. Practice God's math by exchanging addition for multiplication in your ministry.

Consider what I am saying in terms of discipleship. If I mentor 100 people in the course of my life and they continue to follow the Lord, then I've empowered 100 people to Kingdom work. Not bad. However, if I mentor ten people who, in the following year, mentor three people each, and each group multiplies annually in the same way—look at the shift:

Year One: 10 new disciples for the Kingdom
Year Two: 20 new disciples for the Kingdom
Year Three: 90.
Year Four: 270.
Year Five: 810.

In this example, addition (and superhuman effort) harvested 100 laborers. Multiplication (and Holy Spirit power) harvested hundreds more. Don't be content to add; multiply! Empower and teach others to empower. Mentor and teach others to mentor. In order to do this, you must relinquish control and not be the center of every endeavor. Release people fully and watch how the work increases! Give it away for the sake of Christ!

Multi-apply! This thinking must be applied laterally and in many domains. One of your goals should be about reproducing a variety of ministries everywhere. When someone is ready to trust Christ, allow another who has never led a person in this step take that opportunity instead of you. It is a blessing for you to lead someone to Christ, but it will be absolutely transforming for your friend who has never done it! Equip people to lead a prayer service or the new Bible study—then release them to lead in their own way. A mature, biblically-oriented leader is always thinking this way.

You cannot personally minister to every need of every individual in your fellowship.

Even though you may not have the beginnings of a church yet, let me say it again: You cannot personally minister to every need of every individual in your fellowship. God did not design the church in this way. At the outset of your ministry (or as soon as possible if it's too late for that), find people who have pastoral/shepherding gifts. Some people are willing to get up in the middle of the night to help someone in need.

Pull these individuals aside and ask if they would be willing to participate in a care-giving ministry under your direction. Furthermore, create "one-anothering" ministries under the five-fold equipping model of Ephesians 4:11-13. Keep in mind, however, that your fellowship will be noticing everything you're doing (and not doing). Therefore, pay attention to the following basic relational principles:

- Be kind to people. Jesus loves every person, so treat every person with dignity and respect. I've met very talented and gifted Bible teachers who are not nice people. Humility and simple kindness are powerful attributes in the spiritual realm.

- Do a lot of listening. Active listening is rare. Be counted among the few missionaries who actually practice this artful ministry. When we talk all the time, we are relinquishing a powerful ministry tool.

- Be honest with people. People of integrity (words and actions matching) will follow a missionary of integrity.

- Exhibit courage. Stand with people and, when necessary, set yourself over against them on their behalf.

- Earnestly seek God's prophetic direction. Reading the Bible is not enough. A missionary must hear the Lord's direction for his or her life and ministry.

What do I mean by the prophetic? I am speaking about specific counsel and direction from the Spirit. "And in the church God has appointed first of all apostles, second prophets, third teachers..." (1 Corinthians 12:28). The order here is important. First is the apostolic, which refers to the teachings of the Bible. God will never direct a missionary to move outside the counsel of Scriptures. Second is the prophetic. There is a more specific direction (never outside the sphere of apostolic teaching) that will bring about necessary transition within the life of a team or fellowship. Once the prophetic is discovered in a particular season, begin to teach it systematically.

Moving Forward

Constantly be aware of the dynamics of power and authority—both within your team and the fellowships you lead. Remember that many people have been hurt and even abused by people in positions of authority, so don't be surprised if some of people struggle to trust you. It takes a strong sense of identity and tremendous perseverance to survive this stretch of the wilderness of ministry, but this is strategic terrain that must be taken in the name of Christ. Continue to exemplify servant leadership without abdicating God's call on your life. As you walk in this manner, you'll be living out true biblical leadership and leading others in a life-giving way.

1. This chapter begins with the statement, "Every missionary is a leader." Do you believe this? How does your life reflect your position?

2. Spend part of a team meeting reading aloud the parenthetical Scripture references in the last paragraph on page 69. Which of these verses challenge you the most? Why?

3. Ask God to search your heart: Are you bringing a personal agenda to the life of your team? Talk together about what God impresses on you.

4. What principle presented in this chapter could most help your team at this point in time? Why?

5. Pioneers' InTent leadership training advocates a "cross" approach to mentoring. Leaders need to be mentored by someone above them, pour into someone who is not as far along as they are ("below" them), and also have peer-mentoring relationships that extend horizontally. Draw a cross and name who is in each category for you. Are any categories empty? If so, what will you do about it?

So Christ Himself gave the apostles, the prophets, the evangelists, the pastors and teachers, to equip His people for works of service, so that the body of Christ may be built up until we all reach unity in the faith and in the knowledge of the Son of God and become mature, attaining to the whole measure of the fullness of Christ. — Ephesians 4:11-13

KNOW YOUR MISSION

All authority in heaven and on earth has been given to me. Therefore go and make disciples of all nations, baptizing them in the name of the Father and of the Son and of the Holy Spirit, teaching them to obey everything I have commanded you. And surely I am with you always, to the very end of the age.

— Matthew 28:18-20

The Great Commission is not an option to be considered; it is a command to be obeyed.

— Hudson Taylor

This generation of Christians is responsible for this generation of souls on earth!

— Keith Green

The mark of a great church is not its seating capacity, but its sending capacity.

— Mike Stachura

The Church must send or the church will end.

— Mendell Taylor

I look upon the world as my parish.

—John Wesley

We are called to come to the Lord and be refreshed. We are also called to go into a broken world and make disciples of all nations. This coming and going is a spiritual rhythm, a healthy balance of receiving and giving. The private equipping, refreshing and repair between you and the Lord in your inner sanctuary is vital. Getting out of your church (if it exists) and onto the streets is equally vital. Eliminating one or the other damages the "*shalom*-balance" the Lord desires.

The posture of the Spirit-filled missionary is advancement. After you have learned how to stand in Christ and hold the ground He's given you, God is calling you to take new ground and, in so doing, to set captives free. If you remain in your own castle simply protecting what you have, you become like the servant who buried his one talent.

Your mindset about safety must change. A conservative approach is not necessarily safer. A strategy of non-advancement is not necessarily less risky. When God calls us to advance, the safest place is to advance. When God calls us to pull back, the safest place is to pull back. It is less risky walking on the water with Jesus than remaining huddled under a blanket in the boat without Him.

With that said, it is imperative for every missionary to realize that advancement is the normal posture for the church. The enemy is always looking for ways to invade. The best defense consists of a powerful offense that moves into his territory. Keep the enemy on the move by speaking the Word of God and developing an advancement mindset in those you serve.

The private equipping, refreshing and repair between you and the Lord in your inner sanctuary is vital.

God is the original pioneer. He is on the move and wants you to move with Him. Some missionaries become lethargic and comfortable as they grow older. After 20 or 30 years in ministry, these missionaries should be the most outrageous, excited, Spirit-filled dreamers on the face of the earth. Instead, boredom has set in. Their ministry has become like old manna—worm-ridden and without nourishment. I love meeting missionaries who are chronologically older but have youthful hearts. They are captivated by God's love. They are not afraid to take adventures with the Lord.

Become captivated by a holy restlessness, thirsty for new terrain and new discoveries. Allow His wonderment to embrace your heart.

S T R E T C H in the way you relate to others. Are you married? Do you have children? When the Spirit of God releases you into a mindset of advancement, they will recognize the change immediately. Your desire to learn, to discover, to listen, to dream, to actively invest and pursue more deeply will radically change the dynamics of your home life.

> *Become captivated by a holy restlessness, thirsty for new terrain and new discoveries.*

As the mindset of advancement becomes more pronounced in you, every relationship on your team will be impacted too. You will begin to hear the language and dreams of advancement rising up in conversations. That's when you know the new wine is finally being caught in something other than the old, inflexible wineskins.

The mindset of advancement is exciting, but there is a cost. In order to advance, you must be willing to leave the old and let go of the familiar—even if you've already done that more than once in your missionary career. You might not like it. It's like hiking a new trail; you don't know exactly what comes next, or what you will find around the next bend. It could lead to the most incredible view ever or you could get lost and have to retrace your steps. To advance, you must be willing to risk.

But there is also a significant cost that comes with a mindset of non-advancement. While you are working hard to protect and maintain the status quo of your life and ministry, your heart is dying a slow death—the death of non-adventure that comes from breathing stale spiritual air.

Jesus said, "Whoever wants to save his life will lose it, but whoever loses his life for me will save it" (Luke 9:24). You've lived this by choosing to be a missionary, but the command doesn't stop there. Be willing to advance to wherever he calls,

Be willing to advance to wherever he calls, avoiding status quo life and ministry at all cost.

avoiding status quo life and ministry at all cost. Stop spending your time protecting what you have. Instead, give yourself away. Adventure with God. Journey with Him in the wild terrain. Breath in the fresh air. Chase after the Poem that can only be heard outside the confines of the castle gate.

Develop also a mindset of advancement concerning your own personhood. Be open to new experiences in your daily journey with the Lord. Allow God's creativity to breathe life into your spiritual disciplines. Be innovative and inquisitive in your pursuit of knowledge. Be willing to read new books and explore new thoughts! Try fasting for three days and nights. Spend a week without talking. Embark on a vision quest to a secluded location. Spend a year studying the Song of Songs. Learn a new language. Challenge the familiar. Tear up your old maps. Chart new terrain in the name of Jesus. Look at the ocean of ministry; it is so expansive. Venture out onto the open sea!

Advancing from Talk to Walk

The mindset of advancement must give birth to structural change. A proper foundation is essential if your team is to be a force for the Kingdom. God has a divine design for communities of faith. Decide right now that you will not settle for second best. You are going to have to clear the rubble field and dig deep in order to do foundational work. When you start making adjustments on a foundational level, the whole building will be shaken. God shakes everything. He wants you to see what will fall out and what sticks.

Of course, not everything is up for grabs. The principles of Scriptures are unchanging as is God's character. The mission of the church—to continue the work that Jesus began in

His earthly ministry through the power of His Spirit—may change in form, but not in its ultimate goal of salvation and justice for all.

Our faith contains a healthy tension between that which is to never change and that which must change. As Eugene Peterson states, "We want a Christian faith that has stability but is not petrified; [one] that has vision but is not hallucinatory."[14] Be discerning in this regard as you move forward in community.

Establish right priorities: His Kingdom, His culture, His way and His will—not ours. Establish proper alignment: God first, Kingdom work first. Feelings and comfort need to be way down on the list if they figure into it at all. Right structures need to be set in place.

We advance on our knees. We move forward on our faces. The fiercest battle takes place in the realm of intercession. Prayer covering is vital. Advancement begins when a missionary chooses to be unashamedly devoted to meeting with God.

Advancement begins when a missionary chooses to be unashamedly devoted to meeting with God.

Intimacy with God and desperation for a move of God are the prerequisites for change. Missionary, once your lifestyle is aligned with the will of God in this regard, begin building an army of intercessors. Intercession is foolishness to the world. Pray for such foolishness in the churches you plant. Pray for tenaciously foolish people who will stand with you in the spiritual wilderness to which God has called you.

Advancing Into the New

Imagine a farmer working diligently in his fields. From dawn until dusk, he labors to produce a harvest. But instead of planting seed, he's planting grains of sand. This is fruitless work. All his labor, all his investment of time and energy, all the water and nutrients will amount to nothing. He cannot produce a harvest from a grain of sand. He needs good seed.

What's the good seed?
Nothing but Jesus!
Nothing but the fire!
Nothing but radical discipleship!
Nothing but Acts 2 leading to Matthew 28!

Seek after the Presence of God. Chase after and then remain in His Presence. Strength, inspiration, courage, joy, anointing—all flow from being in His Presence. Without the pillar of fire, the Tabernacle is nothing more than a tent. Without the Presence of God, our worship is nothing more than empty religion. Plant seed, not sand.

Beware of fruitless vines. They look so healthy! They expand over great areas, taking precious nutrients to feed themselves, yet they produce no fruit. Don't hesitate to take the ax and cut them off at the root.

Beware of fruitless meetings: Doing the same things the same way does not make sense if no eternal fruit comes from it. Break up the fallow ground: Turn the weeds over and refresh the soil.

> *Doing the same things the same way does not make sense if no eternal fruit comes from it.*

If the pillar of fire is not over the Tent of Meeting, pray and pray and fast and pray until the fire appears—because apart from the Presence of God, your presence among your unreached people group is powerless and lost.

Beware of fruitlessness!

Beware of fruitless words. Words that are repeated again and again yet produce no eternal fruit need to be eliminated from your vocabulary.

Beware of fruitless associations, partnerships and friendships. The Spirit of God wants to plant an orchard in your life for His glory. Don't fill up the acreage with fruitless endeavors.

Clear the field! After fasting and praying, after getting clear direction from the Lord, clear the land! Do the hard work. Bring out the chain saw and the stump grinder. Pile up the dead branches on the side of the field. Clear the rubble out of the way. Then bring in the plow. Be careful to plant good seed. God will be faithful and cause the growth.

One more word about change: Be thankful if your team is in transition and being stretched. The most frightening prospect is the team that has become dormant and is dying a slow, cold death. Keep the fires burning! Embrace change. Introduce variations in strategy as well as worship and prayer times. Glance at the past, but focus on the future. Let people see the unfolding vision of the Kingdom of God advancing in your unreached area.

Advancing Beyond Your Current Area

The Lord is concerned not only about those in your focus group, but also about "Jerusalem, Judea, Samaria and the ends of the earth" (Acts 1:8). The two spheres must connect. The church among your unreached group—no matter how small—must ultimately develop a mission vision to survive. If you focus only on your unreached people group, your ministry will not flourish under God's greater blessing.

From this new perspective, the work in the garden seemed strangely ingrown and myopic.

A few years ago, I believe the Lord gave me the following picture:

> *I envisioned a field being farmed. A small portion of the field was being fertilized and watered—it was like a garden. The larger portion of the field was ignored.*

> *Even though there were many workers in the small garden, it seemed as if they were laboring in vain. Ten people were gathered around two or three plants, not just for minutes, but for days at a time. I continued to watch the work of these people even though I was disturbed by what I saw.*

> *The Lord asked me to lift up my eyes and look around. I looked*

up and saw the expanse of land surrounding this small garden plot. There were acres and acres of farmland, most of it uncultivated. From this new perspective, the work in the garden seemed strangely ingrown and myopic.

I asked one of the workers why this small garden was receiving so much attention when the fields surrounding it were receiving none. He answered, "Every time we pass by this plot, the plants scream and cry out for more food, water and attention. They seem so full of pain and misery that all of us become deeply concerned for their welfare. We work to quench their thirst and desire to see them grow. Before long, the sun is setting and we realize that we've spent another full day in the garden."

He came to the crowded garden area, knelt down and tenderly touched each emaciated plant.

"Does the garden seem to benefit from all your labor?" I asked.

"That's the strangest thing," the other said. "With all this attention, one would think that this garden would be flourishing. But I'm beginning to think that all our support is making these plants weaker rather than stronger."

"What about these other fields?" I asked. "Are they not also the property of the One who owns the garden?"

"Yes, and we are certain he wants us to farm that land also. But if we are unable to cause this little garden to grow, how can we move on to a more expansive mission?"

Our conversation ended abruptly as the Owner Himself walked towards us. He had chosen this day to inspect the work in His fields. He came to the crowded garden area, knelt down and tenderly touched each emaciated plant.

"These plants must choose whether or not they want to flourish," He said. "They have grown dependent upon all your service and have not yet been given an opportunity to decide for themselves whether or not they want to enter into the work of living and *producing fruit for others. You do well to continue caring for them, but only to the extent that you care for the rest of the field."*

Then I watched the Owner stand up and look at the fields around Him. His eyes moved across the acres of land that had remained untouched in this season. The farm workers and I naturally began to look where He was looking, and we began to see what He was seeing.

All of this land; uncultivated, untouched, uncared for.

The Owner was silent as He gazed over the fields. The waiting was uncomfortable. Then His gaze fell upon us.

"How has this happened?" He asked. "How is it that these fields have received nothing from your hand? Was it not clear that I placed all of these fields under your supervision?"

The workers nodded. The Owner called them to come closer. He laid His hands on the shoulders of the ones nearest Him. Tenderly, yet sternly, He said, "My friends, what I require of you is obedience to My commands. The growth of the plants and the size of the harvest are in many ways beyond your control, but your obedience is not. There are many voices telling you to 'Come here' and 'Do this,' but it is My voice you must obey. Pledge to Me now that you will faithfully work in all the fields that I have set before you. And when I return for My next inspection, I will be able to say, 'Well done, good and faithful servant!'"

The journey to the fields is less about technique and more about stepping out of one's comfort zone.

The workers pledged their commitment anew, and so did I.

It is not comfortable to lift our eyes and see all of the fields we have not cultivated. It is not easy to watch the Master's eyes as he looks over the neighborhoods, the schools, the streets, the towns that He has place under our supervision, but this is the first incision of His scalpel into our hearts. It is our awakening to look beyond our small garden.

Many missionaries are not comfortable in their own skin. Some of us simply don't know how to "be" with people. Do you want to learn? Are you willing to be a beginner? This new mindset will require courage. The journey to the fields is less about technique and more about stepping out of one's comfort zone.

Don't wait for a quiet day. If we wait for things to settle down in our ministries, we might as well abandon all hope of ever making it to the fields. The time has come to be proactive. Schedule part of every day (even if its 30 minutes) for "field" work. Explore! Let me state it again: God is a pioneer and He wants us to join Him in His adventure of reaching the lost and mending what has been broken.

Go to the streets of your town. Sit down on a bench. Ask the Lord for His vision for the acres and acres of uncultivated land. If you ask Him, He will give you opportunities to stretch. Keep entering into conversations with people you've never met. There are millions of "strangers" in the world. Once you learn to break through the "stranger barrier," a whole new terrain of ministry is available to you!

The primary work is the shift in the core of our beings.

As a missionary, you're well aware of the need to be a student of the culture in order to reach a culture. How precious is the missionary who learns to speak French in order to be taught Wolof! How beautiful is the commitment of the missionary who studies Arabic for five years in order to effectively reach out to those on the Arabian Peninsula. Even in these locations, decide today to cross over the stranger barrier and work outside the garden gate.

Our daily schedules are an outward manifestation of an inward work. The primary work is the shift in the core of our beings. We must determine within ourselves that we will no longer focus only on the garden—even if it is part of the uncultivated field to the rest of the world. We need to have big picture vision for the completion of the Great Commission and not just for one portion of it.

Moving Forward

Missionary, promote the cause of missions with new followers of Jesus early in their discipleship process. We are created in the image of God and therefore created to receive *and* give. Encourage them to be evangelists in their own community, but also among unreached peoples of the world.

CHAPTER 7 STUDY QUESTIONS

1. For your team, who is your "field"?

2. What are you doing to think about advancement? (e.g. prayer, team prayer, prayer walking, team discussions, team retreats, talking and praying with other leaders) Ask your team how they feel about the team's advancement.

3. Who are you focusing on now? How long has that been your focus? Is it time for a change in focus?

4. Reread the author's story in italics on pages 83-85. Would the Lord give you a picture (in whatever form He chooses) of what He thinks of your team's focus and work at the moment?

5. Are you a visionary? If so, are you verbalizing your vision and getting input from others on it? If you are not a visionary, how are you tapping into others who could give you new thoughts?

REMEMBER THE
JOY OF THE LORD

Joy, which was the small publicity of the pagan, is the gigantic secret of the Christian.

— G.K. Chesterton

The Bible says, "Do not grieve, for the joy of the Lord is your strength" (Nehemiah 8:10). I have found this to be true: Without God's joy, I would be overcome by fear, anxiety and responsibility. The task is too great and the burden is too heavy for me in my own strength. God, however, has a secret weapon for us; He wants to fill us up with His joy!

It was the joy of the Lord the caused Ignatius, in the year A.D. 110, to appeal to the Church of Rome not to deliver him from martyrdom "because they would deprive him of that which he most longed and hoped for."[15] It was the joy of the Lord that caused Perpetua to see her dungeon as a palace.[16] It was the same infilling that caused Cyril, "the 84-year-old bishop of the church at Gortyna to display no fear when Lucius condemned him to be burned at the stake, and [he] suffered the flames joyously and with great courage."[17]

Richard Wurmbrand writes: "When I look back on my fourteen years in prison, it was occasionally a very happy time. Other prisoners and even the guards very often wondered at how happy Christians could be under the most terrible circumstances."[18]

Not many of us have had to endure such hardship, yet many believers live defeated and joyless lives. Certainly the pressure is real. The ministry, at times, can be overwhelming,

97

but God doesn't want his ambassadors walking around like they are barely in the ranks of the living. He wants to shock the world by shining His joy through our broken lives.

Recently, the Lord showed me that I had lost my childlikeness. In a very gentle way, He revealed that years before, I smiled and laughed more. The cares of the world, my compassion for hurting people, the intensity of ministry—all had become a heavy yoke on my shoulders. The Lord was showing me that He was delighted that I cared so deeply for people, but that my testimony was not complete without His joy pouring through me. I began crying out for an anointing of joy, peace and power in my life and ministry. I asked God to deliver me from looping thoughts that were leading me around the same mountain and filling me with heaviness and despair.

I am actively cooperating with the Lord concerning the renewing of my mind; I don't want discouraging and frustrating thoughts to steal away my testimony of joy in this broken and frenetic world. The world is searching for joy, yet apart from Christ, all that can be found is a temporary diversion. God's intention is that, when our neighbors look at us, they will see a deeper, more permanent joy springing up in our lives.

Karl Barth, author of a six million word, 12-volume work on dogmatics (plus 40 or 50 other books), wrote: "The theologian who has no joy in his work is not a theologian at all. Sulky faces, morose thoughts and boring ways of speaking are intolerable in this science."

We must learn the secret that has been the battle cry of millions of believers throughout history: "The joy of the Lord is my strength!" When circumstances press in on you, remember who lives inside of you and rejoice! When you are weary because of the burden on your shoulders, remember who lives inside of you and rejoice. When you are placed in the fiery furnace and, in the natural, there doesn't seem to be a way of escape, remember who walks with you and rejoice. God's joy has miracle working power. Grab onto it and don't let it go. In His strength we can do amazing things!

Final Word and Blessing

Missionary, thank you for your ministry to the body of Christ and for your witness to the world! My prayer is that you have been strengthened and encouraged by the words in this book. If you have received any helpful insights, inspiration or refreshment from these pages, I am honored and blessed to have served you in the name of our Lord Jesus Christ. This is our time to shine. We are on this earth for only a moment and have been blessed with a great commissioning. We have been given a great gospel to proclaim and are empowered with the Holy Spirit.

I am praying that you stand your post and don't back away. I pray that the joy of the Lord will be your strength and that Jesus Himself will give you wisdom to equip and prepare the people you serve for Kingdom advancement. Continue standing, continue running and continue dreaming!

"To him who is able to keep you from falling and to present you before his glorious presence without fault and with great joy—to the only God our Savior be glory, majesty, power and authority, through Jesus Christ our Lord, before all ages, now and forevermore" (Jude 24-25)!

Amen.

A SURVIVAL KIT FOR THE DESERT

B uild this kit (in the form of a file, a box or whatever works for you) immediately; continue to add to it and have it within reach always.

A Confidant: Include the name of at least one confidant outside your team. Have his/her phone number in your survival kit. This means the person understands his/her mission and has given you permission to call at any time. The relationship must be developed and maintained so that when you find yourself in the desert without many options, this will be a lifeline.

A Retreat Option: Have an agreement with your supervisors—that if things get very intense you have permission to request three or four days away without having to "sell" the idea to them. Verbalize your commitment to offer an explanation after your retreat. Do not use this option unless you are truly in the desert. Have a place arranged—not too far (but far enough), not too expensive (but have money saved for the occasion).

A Declaration Paper: Include a declaration paper in your survival kit—a list of declarations that speak to your identity and destiny. These affirmations are written in the good times so that when all is crashing around you and you find yourself in the desert place, the words will provide an oasis of protection from the deep arrows of the enemy.

Two or Three Important Letters from friends: include in your survival kit a few letters/e-mails that bless you in a special way and that confirm your call.

Prophetic Pictures (that have been confirmed) and Life Verses: Have these handy—written out and in your file labeled "Desert Survival Kit."

Procedural Commitments: Write down how you will make decisions while in the desert, and do not surrender to your feelings in this season. Examples:

- I will pray before acting.

- I will seek counsel from two to three different sources.

- I will not act independently. I will walk in community.

- I will fast.

- I will wait on the Lord and be careful to hear what He's saying to me.

- I will journal.

Prepare this survival kit, and know where it is at all times. Continue to add to it as the Lord gives you wisdom. Believe me, this will be a welcome friend numerous times in your ministry career.

THE IDENTITY SCHOOL FOR CHRISTIAN MINISTRY

I f you are interested in further study concerning surviving and thriving in ministry, consider attending a Spiritual Survival Workshop for Cross-Cultural Workers, a course by the Identity School for Christian Ministry that is designed specifically for missionaries. The course unpacks each of the chapter topics, adding new material to reinforce the principles of "ministry survivalism." Each intensive five-day seminar is an interactive time of learning and seeking the Lord. Whether you're preparing to leave for your first term, or are returning to your field of service, this course is a great opportunity to shore up spiritually.

To learn more about The Identity School for Christian Ministry, visit *theidentityschool.com.*

FOR TEAM LEADERS

When we begin as team leaders we believe we are on board with God's agenda—an agenda to reach a lost people group, a lost city and to help build His church. This is indeed His agenda, but it isn't His only one. He has another agenda. One that feels often like it is competing with the one we already own, but which in reality is there to enhance it. This agenda is to invest our lives into a group of teammates so that as a healthy team His work can be accomplished and His love shown. Sometimes this investment takes much sacrifice—a laying down of our own "work" in order that our efforts might be multiplied in others. These teammates aren't there just as tools to be utilized in completing our vision. They are there to be loved and related to. They are there to refine us and for us to refine them. They are present not to strain us or frustrate us, but to more fully represent Jesus in our location than we could ever do by ourselves. By embracing this reality we honor God, honor our calling and are engaged in the charge given to Peter which is also given to us—"Feed my sheep."

— a missionary in Asia

Who is on the throne of your heart? If your feelings, opinions, wisdom or personal agendas drive you, your heart has shifted from being Christ-governed to being self-governed. When the enemy sees the lack of complete surrender in a team leader's heart, that is when he will pounce. Do not give him any ground. Remember survival key number one, and be absolutely vigilant regarding the posture of your own heart. Only then can you walk in true servant leadership authority as a team leader. What does this look like?

In their book, *The Subtle Power of Spiritual Abuse*, David Johnson and Jeff VanVonderen wrote, "Spiritual abuse can occur when a leader uses his or her spiritual position to control or dominate another person. It often involves overriding the feelings and opinions of another, without regard to what will result in the other person's state of living, emotions or spiritual well-being."[19]

"Power-over" leadership is not biblical. We are not called to be the Caesars of a kingdom, but servants of the King. Some team leaders are on power trips, loving the attention of being the so-called "head." Any use of the leadership office to coerce, impose or manipulate is an abuse of power and is not of the Spirit of God.

On the other hand, I tell you from experience that a vacuum of authority is just as dangerous as an over-reaching or control-ling authority. When a team leader does not lead, something or someone else will attempt to fill the void. Anarchy comes in a variety of forms—none of them are good. More importantly, no form of anarchy is biblical. God has called you to lead your team. Until that call changes, do so gently but without apology.

There is a grasping for power—like the first Adam who reached out to be like God. Then there is a power that surrenders, like the second Adam, "who in very nature God, did not consider equality with God something to be grasped" (Philippians 2:6). Do not grasp! At the same time, do not abdicate your position of authority and step away from the place where the Spirit has you standing.

You will need to develop a high level of discernment with regard to issues of leadership authority. Some people crave it, others fear it, but every person is impacted by it. Learn all you can about how power operates in systems. Become a student of its subtleties. In this way, you can help prevent abuse, manipula-tion and other destructive uses of power in relationship.

True spiritual authority is not haughty and loud. It is not about theological degrees or the titles on a business card. It is derived from a life hidden in Christ and lived out in strict obedience to

God's call. Those who are not spiritually discerning will not honor true authority no matter what you do. I'm saying this to you now so that when you are disrespected without cause, you will not be discouraged. However, people who are grounded in the Word will respect this kind of spiritual authority and will not settle for the worldly counterfeit.

Team Meetings

Team meetings, in whatever format, are a vital venue for you to exercise spiritual leadership. The regular agenda can be a battleground. The urgent always screams for attention. Learn to delegate so that you can move forward with essential discussions on strategy, the Word and prayer. After praying, look over the agenda and start with the items you and your team feel are of utmost priority.

Remember to include items that focus on God's prophetic direction and the enemy's attacks. Seek consensus in decision-making. Encourage all members of the team to speak their hearts and leave everything at the table. If the discussion gets bogged down, step away from it, pray together and try again. The tendency will always be to trust your own understanding. Learn to use your spiritual gifts instead.

The enemy will constantly attack the unity of your team. Be alert to subtle relational dynamics; have a keen eye for anyone distancing themselves from the team. Push to resolve unsettled discussions and hurt feelings. Don't allow distance to creep in.

There will be seasons when a particular teammate frustrates you. Do not speak inappropriately about this teammate, even to someone else on the team. Be careful how you express your frustration. Go directly to the person with whom you're struggling. Treat every person the way you would want to be treated. Have the conversations you need to have, but have them in a straightforward and honoring way. Walk with integrity.

Don't be sloppy and casual in team meetings. Rather, be fully prepared and full of light. Awaken and inspire your team.

Bring insights that God is revealing to you through His word. Suggest books that provoke and challenge new thought. Stir up the gifts of your team. Encourage them.

Establish a Prayer Base

Do you have two or three true intercessors on your team? If so, you have been truly blessed by the Lord! Call on them and ask them to pray for your survival. Ask them to intercede daily for you, your family, the team and the people to which you've been called. This is the initial hedge of protection in the spiritual realm. From this beginning point, you can extend outward and advance for His glory. Meet with this small team regularly. Encourage them. Give them general prayer points. Pour into them. The Lord has placed them as your guards in the spiritual realm.

Prayer is the deepest, most intimate spiritual discipline. When this work is being accomplished, ministry begins to accelerate, but so do the attacks. The enemy is not concerned about plastic Christianity, but when believers fall on their knees and cry out desperately for God's Kingdom to come, the demons are stirred up like a hornet's nest.

The "simple" decision to establish regular team times of prayer is huge in the spiritual realm. Attacks will come from every direction. You have set a stake and the enemy will snarl at you. You have made a declaration to move forward into battle and not play at ministry.

There are teams that set aside every Tuesday as a day of prayer and fasting. Others struggle to keep prayer a part of regular meetings. After one missionary learns the language well, he devotes the hours he'd have spent in language learning to prayer instead. Another missionary can't remember the last time she had quality time with God. What makes the difference? One missionary has become convinced that apart from God's intervention his life will amount to nothing. The other missionary actually believes more in human effort than the gospel itself.

Do we really believe that apart from Him we can do nothing? Do we really believe that intimacy with Christ is at the heart of transformation? Such conviction will drive us to our knees and we will devote ourselves to the wonderful discipline of prayer. At the very beginning, decide that your team will be a praying team.

Prayer times open our eyes to the truth about God and the truth about ourselves: that God is great and we are not. We need Him. A mindset of desperation begins to emerge within a praying team. Choose this day to be a team leader who both practices and promotes prayer. Apart from the Spirit of God we can do nothing of eternal consequence.

The arguments against setting this pattern can be articulate and reasonable:

> *People are so busy! I don't want to overburden them.*

> *I can't commit to everything; I need to have time to minister to my family.*

> *Of course prayer is important, but why do we need to come together? Why can't we all pray individually from our homes as God calls us to pray?*

Keep your position simple and steadfast: God desires us to be a praying community (Luke 19:46, Acts 2:42, 1 Thessalonians 5:17). The culture you serve will not change apart from your team moving together. It pleases God when we gather in His name to seek His face.

Everyone believes prayer is good! It is not a theological issue; it is a question of commitment and convenience. Fight to make prayer a priority on your team. Then, move to advance the Kingdom of God with the power of the Holy Spirit!

Structuring the Weekly Prayer Meeting

Prayer is strategic for advancement, so expect the enemy to interfere in any way he can. Typical methods are distraction, offense, carnal spirituality and tardiness. To diffuse them, prepare for your prayer meetings ahead of time. Have an "agenda" for the prayer meeting, but always leave space for something unexpected. Place prayer needs on PowerPoint. Break out of the traditional "one at a time" praying method and ask people to intercede all at once for any of the requests before them.

I believe it is important to pray over particular domains of ministry. The structure of a prayer meeting will, in and of itself, be instructional for your team. Think in terms of personal transformation, team transformation and societal and global transformation.

Open with global as often as possible because it is healthy to begin with an outward focus. Take five or ten minutes and pray for missionaries in other regions of the world, a persecuted country or a current crisis situation in the world (earthquake, flood, famine).

Team transformation might include prayer for relationships, strategy or leadership. Every ministry of your team needs to be bathed in prayer. All three areas of transformation may not be covered every week, so it is important to rotate through the month, as all these areas are vital and need consistent intercession.

It is important that individual team members requesting prayer can receive it at some point in the meeting. Mobilize your team to pray for one another. Instruct your team in the principle of take and give by saying, "This week, you may need to receive. Next week, perhaps you will be the one who can give." Both are valid parts of ministry.

Beyond this structure, add in worship and a time of waiting on the Lord. Give brief instruction on what you're looking for at particular times in the prayer meeting. Sometimes people want to move as a unit but just don't know what to do, so give them clear expectations and boundaries.

In the regular prayer meeting, it is important to talk less and pray more. The reason you are gathered is to meet with God as a team. Pray for His manifest presence to fill your meeting space. Jesus is interceding for each of us in the heavenly tabernacle. Strive to hear His prayers and then pray them for one another according to the Spirit. Beware of people who want to dominate the prayer time. Instruct your team not to "fill" the time with many things. Linger in worship and adoration like Mary and intercede with the rigor of Martha. Always remember that worship and prayer perform a beautiful sacred dance before the King of Kings.

Monthly Prayer Vigils

I have learned from our African brothers and sisters how powerful an extended time of prayer can be for a team and its ministries. By "extended," I mean starting with at least four hours of prayer. Then, over the first few months, lengthen the vigils. Try a twelve hour vigil one day. Later, try one that extends through the night. Intersperse prayer times with worship. Include all types of prayer; don't be afraid to stretch and experiment. We are about spiritual work so we must approach it spiritually.

Learn from Others

My personal experience comes from a church setting, but veteran cross-cultural workers in Asia concur with what I've presented:

> *The way God reveals Himself in the context of relationship (the Trinity), proves God's value of and our need for community. Healthy teams are rooted in relational connection. In the team context, we join in each other's journeys to provide strengthening, godly perspective, accountability and opportunities for transformation. As a result, the way we relate as a team is a key part of our witness to the community around us and an anchor for ministry. It adds power to the gospel message. How does this look?*

> • *Providing opportunities for prayer, worship and time in the Word as a team is of key importance. Seek to be creative. Let*

each person have opportunities to lead, letting it be an expression of who they are. Make prayer a team priority. Set regular prayer days and periodically spend extended times together in prayer in addition to regular prayer.

- *Second, develop clear team documents that reflect the purpose for God putting your team together and for where He is taking you. Keep reviewing and evaluating this in light of what you are doing at present or have just completed.*

- *Third, teams never outgrow the need for team-building opportunities. Plan events that involve working together toward a goal (including the children), celebration and getting to know each other's hearts.*

- *Fourth, schedule regular times for spiritual and ministry accountability. In addition, provide opportunity as a group for debriefing after key events or travel, victories or defeats, and loss.*

Our teams are community, but they need to also be part of the larger community. It isn't healthy to allow the team to become ingrown. We are part of something much bigger than ourselves.

APPENDIX 3 STUDY QUESTIONS

1. How are you doing as a servant leader? What are your strengths? Weaknesses?

2. Do you struggle more with tendencies toward "power-over" leadership or creating a vacuum of authority? What do you need to work on in either of those tendencies to move more towards being a leader that empowers others?

3. How are you doing at leading your team in meetings? What are you doing to use that time well to empower your team?

4. Who are the intercessors on your team? What are you doing to allow them to contribute their gift to you and your team?

5. What are you doing to establish your team as a praying team? What ideas do you have that will encourage your teammates to be more dependent on the Lord?

END NOTES

Chapter 1

1. Wilderness can mean different things for different people. I have found tremendous encouragement from walking portions of the Appalachian Trail; you may have a garden to which you can retreat, or a park. Others of you may be crying for a spot of green in the urban area where you live. If possible, get away from your routine and into nature.

2. Eldredge, John. *Wild at Heart: Discovering the Secret of a Man's Soul*. Nashville: Thomas Nelson, 2001, 1.

3. I first heard the term "mind-skin" from a teaching offered by Lance Wallnau.

4. Hybels, Bill. *Courageous Leadership*. Grand Rapids: Zondervan, 2002, 29.

Chapter 2

5. Millard, Candice. *The River of Doubt: Theodore Roosevelt's Darkest Journey*. New York: Broadway, 2005, 252.

6. Lewis, C.S. *'Til We Have Faces*. Orlando: Harcourt. 1956, 292.

Chapter 3

7. Lewis, C.S. *The Screwtape Letters*. New York: Harper Collins, 1942, 3.

8. John of the Cross. "Living Flame of Love." Stanza 3.

Chapter 4

9. The Voice of the Martyrs. *The Triumphant Church: A Three-Part Study from the Writings of Richard Wurmbrand, John Piper and Milton Martin*. Bartlesville: VOM, 1999, 4.

10. Bevere, John. *The Bait of Satan*. Lake Mary: Charisma, 1994, 6.

11. Lucado, Max. *Facing Your Giants*. Nashville: W, 2006, 25.

Chapter 5

12. Reccord, Bob. *Beneath the Surface*. Nashville: Broadman & Holman, 2002.

13. Means, Patrick. *Men's Secret Wars*. Grand Rapids: Fleming H. Revell, 1996.

Chapter 7

14. Peterson, Eugene. *A Long Obedience in the Same Direction: Discipleship in an Instant Society*. Downers Grove: InterVarsity, 1980, 159.

Epilogue

15. Foxe, John. *Foxe's Book of Martyrs*. Whitefish: Kessinger, 2004, 14.

16. Foxe, John. *Foxe's Book of Martyrs*. Whitefish: Kessinger, 2004, 20.

17. Foxe, John. *Foxe's Book of Martyrs*. Whitefish: Kessinger, 2004, 24.

18. Wurmbrand, Richard. *Tortured for Christ*. Bartlesville, Living Sacrifice, 1967, 57.

Appendix 3

19. Johnson, David & VanVonderen, Jeff. *The Subtle Power of Spiritual Abuse*. Grand Rapids: Bethany, 1991, 20-21.

ACKNOWLEDGEMENTS

Apart from some very special people in my life, this book would have never been written. Special thanks to Joni, my partner in marriage and soul mate, and for Christie and Dana (my daughter and son)—thank you for your encouragement and support. I love you!

Lucinda Sutton, you provided tremendous editorial support and guidance and remained in the trenches with me. This book is better written because of your prayerful skill and artistry with words! Randy Frame, you came along side of me when few people believed in me. Your guidance and encouragement was invaluable! Thank you for joining me in this venture to encourage missionaries around the world. Brian McCloskey, thank you for serving with your creative skills and joining me in birthing a ministry.

To the elders and congregation of Cornerstone Christian Fellowship: I have the greatest church family in the whole world. Your prayers, encouragement and friendships have inspired me to dream big dreams for the Kingdom of God.

I am indebted to my mentors: Dr. Manfred Brauch, Drs. Peter and Carol Schreck, and Dr. Glenn Koch.

I am dedicating this book to missionaries on the front lines. Stand strong! I believe in you and am thankful for your ministry to the Body of Christ.